CW01653612

© D. C. Thomson & Co., Ltd. 1987
ISBN 0 85116 393 9

£2.80

Victor
BOOK FOR BOYS 1988
A 97

CONTENTS

Printed and Published in Great Britain by
D. C. THOMSON & CO., LTD., 185 Fleet Street, London EC4A 2HS.

A TOUGH TEST FOR ALF TUPPER
When Alf Tupper, the famous runner known as the Tough of the Track, read a newspaper article about a curious, old running record, he decided to have a crack at beating it. Alf went to Breconfield and was earning his keep by doing odd welding jobs . . .
THERE YOU ARE, MR SMEDLEY, GOOD AS NEW. IF I CAN JUST CLEAN UP I'LL BE ON MY WAY. I WANT TO CHECK ON SOME FACTS AT YOUR LOCAL LIBRARY.
HAVE A BITE TO EAT WITH US BEFORE YOU GO, LAD.
I SAW AN ARTICLE ABOUT AN OLD RUNNING RECORD IN THE LOCAL PAPER. IT APPEARS YOU USED TO HAVE AN ANNUAL RACE IN BRECONFIELD FOR THE CLAPPER CLOCK — WHATEVER THAT IS. I PLAN TO WIN IT!
WIN THE CLAPPER CLOCK? YOU? OH, DEAR!
A LOT OF THESE OLD VILLAGE CUSTOMS HAVE DIED OUT, LAD. IT MUST BE SEVENTY YEARS SINCE ANYONE RACED FOR THE CLAPPER CLOCK!
THAT'S WHY I WANT TO GET ALL THE GEN FROM THE LOCAL LIBRARY, MR SMEDLEY. THANKS FOR THE SANDWICH!
BUT THE MAN IS A COMPLETE STRANGER, GEORGE! DO YOU REALISE WHAT THIS COULD MEAN?
I'LL CALL THE MAJOR AT ONCE, CONNIE! WE MUST ARRANGE AN EMERGENCY MEETING OF THE COUNCIL!
LIBRARY
HERE'S THE LIBRARY. I'LL SEE IF I CAN DIG OUT SOME TIMES FOR THE CLAPPER CLOCK RACE!

SEEMS THE CLAPPER CLOCK WAS PRESENTED BY CHARLES CLAPPER IN 1877 AS A PRIZE FOR ANYONE SETTING A NEW RECORD TIME FOR THE BRECONFIELD RACE — A SORT OF TRIATHLON. A QUARTER-MILE SWIM, A THREE-MILE BIKE RIDE AND A FIVE-MILE RUN UP BRECON FELL AND BACK! THE LAST WINNER OF THE CLAPPER CLOCK WAS DAVID DOMAN IN 1905 WITH A TIME OF 1 HOUR 14 MINUTES 25 SECONDS!
Alf inspected the clock in the village square . . .
THE CLAPPER CLOCK. PRESENTED TO BRECONFIELD BY SIR DAVID DOMAN, HOLDER OF THE BRECONFIELD RACE RECORD WHICH HAS NEVER BEEN BETTERED SINCE 1905.
HOW ABOUT THAT! WELL, I DON'T WANT THE CLOCK, BUT I'D SURE LIKE A CRACK AT BREAKING THAT RECORD!
Meanwhile at a meeting of the local council . . .
THE CLAPPER CLOCK IS PART OF BRECONFIELD! IT IS OUR HERITAGE! THE THOUGHT OF SOME STRANGER WINNING IT AND TAKING IT AWAY IS UNTHINKABLE!
WE SIMPLY CANNOT LET THIS HAPPEN!
LADIES AND GENTLEMEN! ORDER PLEASE!
DON'T YOU THINK WE ARE OVER-REACTING IN THIS MATTER? THIS TUPPER FELLOW IS PROBABLY NOT SERIOUS ABOUT REVIVING THE OLD BRECONFIELD RACE.
HE'S SERIOUS ALL RIGHT, MAJOR! HE'S OVER IN THE LIBRARY NOW LOOKING OVER THE RECORDS!
I TELL YOU HERE AND NOW THAT WITHOUT THE CLAPPER CLOCK LIFE IN BRECONFIELD WILL GRIND TO A HALT! PEOPLE SET THEIR WATCHES BY IT! THE BUSES RUN BY IT!
MRS SMEDLEY, DO SIT DOWN! LET US CONSIDER THE PROBLEM RATIONALLY.
MY FATHER, THE LATE SIR DAVID DOMAN, WAS A FINE ATHLETE IN HIS DAY. MANY YOUNG ATHLETES TRIED TO BEAT HIS RECORD TIME BUT THEY ALL FAILED! THE CHANCES ARE THIS TUPPER FELLOW WILL FAIL, TOO!
I SAY WE MUST MAKE SURE HE FAILS!
Alf decided to start training . . .
THE FIRST STAGE OF THE RACE IS TO SWIM THE LENGTH OF THE VILLAGE POND AND BACK. GOOD JOB I BROUGHT MY TRUNKS!
NO FISHING

REALLY! FETCH CONSTABLE RAWLINGS AT ONCE!
HERE GOES!
BLOOMIN' ADA! THESE WATER LILIES ARE SLOWING ME DOWN!
AAH!
ALL RIGHT, CHUMMY, WHAT DO YOU THINK YOUR GAME IS? THERE'S NO SWIMMING ALLOWED IN OUR VILLAGE POND!
I'M IN TRAINING FOR THE BRECONFIELD RACE . . .
. . . AND A VILLAGE BYE-LAW STATES THAT ALL COMPETITORS BE ALLOWED TO TRAIN OVER THE STATED COURSE AT ANY TIME! SO PUT THAT IN YOUR NOTEBOOK AND READ IT — CHUMMY!
Alf changed into his running gear . . .
FIFTY PENCE FOR THE LOAN OF YOUR BIKE, SON.
DONE!
NOW A THREE-MILE RACE ROUND THE VILLAGE!

HANDS OFF THE CLAPPER CLOCK! THAT MUST BE OUR SLOGAN, MAJOR! WE MUST SPREAD THE WORD . . . EEEK!
LOOK WHERE YOU'RE GOING, MISSUS!
Later . . .
BLOOMING ADA! THIS LAST PART OF THE RACE REALLY TAKES IT OUT OF YOU!
ONE HOUR AND TWENTY MINUTES! I'M GOING TO HAVE TO CLIP AT LEAST SIX MINUTES OFF THAT TIME IF I'M TO BEAT THE RECORD!
Alf looked for a place to stay . . .
I'M SORRY, YOUNG MAN, WE HAVE NO ROOMS!
BUT YOUR SIGN SAYS VACANCIES!
VACANCIES
WE FORGOT TO TAKE IT DOWN!
THAT'S THE THIRD BOARDING HOUSE WITH NO VACANCIES! I GET THE FEELING THE NATIVES ARE GETTING HOSTILE!
HANDS OFF OUR CLOCK
BLOOMING ADA! MY VAN!
And later . . .
MY MONEY'S GOOD, MATE! I WANT FISH 'N' CHIPS!
I AIN'T SERVING YOU, LAD! YOU AIN'T WELCOME IN BRECONFIELD!
Outside . . .
THE BRECONFIELD COUNCIL HAS PASSED A RESOLUTION SUSPENDING THE BRECONFIELD RACE FOR THE CLAPPER CLOCK, MR TUPPER! SO YOU MAY AS WELL TAKE THIS — THIS VEHICLE OF YOURS AND LEAVE THE VILLAGE!
I'M SORRY, MRS SMEDLEY, BUT I'VE DONE MY HOMEWORK — AND YOU ARE OUT OF ORDER! YOU CAN'T STOP ANYONE FROM RUNNING THE RACE!

I DIDN'T WANT YOUR BLOOMING CLOCK! I ONLY WANTED TO BREAK YOUR RECORD! BUT I'M GOING TO WIN IT NOW, AND I'M GOING TO TAKE IT — IF IT'S THE LAST THING I EVER DO!
Next day, Alf continued his training . . .
BUS STOP
GANGWAY, FOLKS!
THAT'S BETTER! IF I CAN CLIP ANOTHER THREE SECONDS OFF MY SWIM TIME, AND GET MYSELF A DECENT BIKE, I SHOULD DO IT! I'LL BREAK THE RECORD AND WIN THE CLAPPER CLOCK!
SHOULDN'T BE ALLOWED! THE CLAPPER CLOCK BELONGS TO BRECONFIELD!
OUGHT TO BE A LAW AGAINST IT!
Meanwhile . . .
THIS TUPPER FELLOW HAS EVERY RIGHT TO ATTEMPT TO WIN THE CLAPPER CLOCK. WHAT WE MUST DO IS SEE THAT HE FAILS!
WE MUST FIGHT! HANDS OFF THE CLAPPER CLOCK!
TUPPER WILL FIND WE HAVE A FEW TRICKS UP OUR SLEEVES!
I THINK YOU'VE ALL MET MY SON, TERRY. HE'S POPPED DOWN FROM COLLEGE IN ANSWER TO MY S.O.S. HE'S GOING TO RACE AGAINST TUPPER FOR THE CLAPPER CLOCK!
BUT THAT'S WONDERFUL! TERRY HOLDS THE FIVE THOUSAND METRES RECORD AT HIS COLLEGE! AND HE'S A WONDERFUL SWIMMER, TOO!
ONLY TOO PLEASED TO HELP, FOLKS. I'D LIKE TO MEET THIS TUPPER FELLOW, FATHER.
TERRY DOMAN MAY BE A FINE ATHLETE BUT WE CAN'T BE SURE HE'LL BEAT TUPPER!
WE MUST PUT OUR OTHER PLANS INTO OPERATION, MY DEAR!
TUPPER, I'D LIKE YOU TO MEET MY SON, TERRY. HE'LL BE COMPETING AGAINST YOU IN THE RACE TOMORROW.
GREAT! I DIDN'T FANCY RACING BY MYSELF. I'VE HAD TROUBLE FINDING A DECENT BIKE BUT I GOT THIS OFF THE SCRAP HEAP. IT SHOULD BE OKAY ONCE I'VE FINISHED WITH IT!

MAY THE BEST MAN WIN, EH, MATE?
I INTEND TO, OLD CHAP. ER — PERHAPS WHEN YOU'VE WASHED, EH?
TOFFEE-NOSED TWIT! AIN'T SURE WHICH I'LL ENJOY MOST — WINNING THE CLAPPER CLOCK OR BEATING HIM!
The next day . . .
BLOOMING ADA! I DIDN'T KNOW THE WHOLE VILLAGE WAS COMPETING!
ALF TUPPER
YOU DIDN'T THINK WE'D LET YOU TAKE OUR CLOCK WITHOUT A FIGHT, DID YOU, LAD?
RIGHT, LADS, YOU ALL KNOW THE RULES. YOU MUST SWIM THE LENGTH OF THE POND AND BACK, PUT ON YOUR SHOES AND SHIRTS AND RIDE THE CYCLE COURSE. THEN UP BRECON FELL AND BACK. THERE ARE STEWARDS TO POINT THE WAY. GOOD LUCK TO YOU ALL!
NO HARD FEELINGS, OLD CHAP?
NONE AT ALL — OLD CHAP!
ON YOUR MARKS . . . GET SET . . . GO!
COME ON, TERRY! SHOW 'IM HOW!
HERE, GET OUT OF MY WAY!

Meanwhile . . .
ALL CLEAR, GEORGE! DID THE MUSEUM CURATOR OBJECT?
HE WASN'T VERY KEEN, BUT I EXPLAINED IT WAS FOR A GOOD CAUSE!
I GET IT NOW, YOU LITTLE PERISHERS. YOU WERE PUT IN THE RACE JUST TO HOLD ME BACK!
I CAN'T GET THROUGH 'EM, SO I'LL GO UNDER 'EM!
BLOOMING TWISTERS! THEY KNOCKED ME BACK VITAL MINUTES ON THE SWIM!
HERE, WHAT'S THIS? WHERE'S MY BIKE?
YOU SAID YOU'D HAD TROUBLE FINDING A DECENT MACHINE, TUPPER! WE THOUGHT WE'D HELP OUT! HA, HA, HA!
ALF TUPPER
IF YOU THINK THIS WILL STOP ME YOU'VE GOT ANOTHER THINK COMING! AARGH!

Alf persevered . . .
THIS AIN'T SO BAD WHEN YOU GET THE HANG OF IT!
LOOK OUT! NO BRAKES!
OOF! HOW ARE WE DOING FOR TIME, MATE?
THIRTY-FIVE MINUTES GONE, LAD!
JUST OVER THIRTY-NINE MINUTES LEFT! BUT THIS IS MY SPORT NOW! I'LL RUN 'EM!
BE SURE AND GET YOUR MARK AT THE TOP, LAD, OR YOU'LL BE DISQUALIFIED!
THERE GOES THAT DOMAN TOFF ABOUT THREE MINUTES AHEAD OF ME!

DON'T FORGET YOUR MARK, TUPPER! OOPS! SORRY!
BLOOMING ADA!
Alf pulled out all the stops, and in the home straight . . .
COME ON, TERRY! HE'S CATCHING YOU! RUN, LAD! RUN!
ONE HOUR, FOURTEEN MINUTES, TWELVE SECONDS! TUPPER'S BROKEN THE RECORD! HE WINS THE CLAPPER CLOCK!
Alf let the villagers sweat, and the next day . . .
HOLD IT, FELLERS! I'VE DECIDED THE CLOCK'S TOO BIG FOR THE SIDEBOARD! YOU CAN KEEP IT — BUT THERE IS SOMETHING YOU CAN DO FOR ME!
Later . . .
HOW DO YOU LIKE THE PLAQUE, TUPPER?
JUST FINE, MAJOR!
CLAPPER CLOCK RACE RECORD BROKEN BY ALFRED TUPPER "HE RAN EM"
FOR HE'S A JOLLY GOOD FELLOW, FOR HE'S A JOLLY GOOD FELLOW!
The End

FIGARO!
YEAH! IT IS ME... ZE CLEVER, BRAVE, MODEST FIGARO!
A PICK, A SHOVEL, SOME DIRT ON MY HANDSOME FACE, AN' I IS ALL SET TO FOOL A WHOLE TOWN! JUST WATCH!
GOLD! GOLD! I HAS STRUCK GOLD IN ZE HILLS! I IS RICH!
HEAR WHAT THAT STRANGER SAID? GOLD IN THE HILLS!
SALOON
TO THE GOLD!
WE'LL ALL BE RICH!
SEE? I HAS STARTED A GOLD RUSH! ZE TOWN IS EMPTY! WHAT FOOLS!
EVEN ZE BANK STAFF HAS GONE... BUT I WILL TAKE CARE OF ZE BANK'S CASH!
BANK
SAFE
NO MONEYS LYIN' AROUND! IT MUST ALL BE IN ZE SAFE!
NOTHIN' BUT I.O.U's! WHAT A CHEAP BANK! I'LL BREAK INTO ONE OF ZE HOUSES AN' STEAL SOME CASH!
I.O.U.
WONDER WHERE ZE CASH IS KEPT IN THIS HOUSE?
H'MM! NOT IN ZE WARDROBE!
AN' NOT ON TOP OF ZE WARDROBE!
OH-OH, READERS! YOUR BRAVE HERO IS IN TROUBLE!
YOU SAID IT, FIGARO!
HOI, WARDROBE! LET ME OUTS!
DON'T WORRY, READERS! BRILLIANT FIGARO IS NOT BEATEN YET! I SHOOTS MY WAY OUTS!
I IS SUCH A RUTHLESS BANDIT, NO WARDROBE CAN HOLD ME!
MAYBE THERE IS MONEYS HID UNDER ZE FLOOR.
NO, NOTHING THERE! HUH! THIS IS BEGINNING TO GET ME DOWN!
AARGH! IT HAS GOT ME DOWN!
GRR! THAT IS ZE LAST STRAWBERRY! I IS LEAVIN' THIS USELESS TOWN! GLAD I SENT THEM ALL ON THAT FALSE GOLD RUSH!
BUT OUT IN THE STREET......
GOSH, THANKS FOR THE TIP, STRANGER! THIS USED TO BE THE POOREST TOWN IN THE WEST... BUT NOT NOW!
EH? WHAT YOU MEANS?
WE FOUND THE GOLD IN THE HILLS, JUS' LIKE YOU SAID! WE CLEANED OUT EVERY GRAIN, AN' NOW THIS IS THE RICHEST TOWN IN THE WEST... GOSH! HE'S FAINTED!
GOLD

SPORTS CROSSWORD

CLUES ACROSS

7. A lot of 24 across is played in this country (8)
8. Muhammed Ali took the title from him (6)
10. There's always a point to this kind of match (6)
11. Like a skater's pond — or some football grounds in winter (4,4)
12. Is Jerry one of America's head golfers?
13. This British boxer fought Rocky Marciano for the World Heavyweight title— and lost! (3,7)
15. West Bromwich — or Rovers! (6)
16. Does this type of weight-lifting have to be done in a hurry? (6)
18. A runner will break no records at this rate (6,4)
21. The cold variety of 24 across is played here (4)
22. Will these deliveries make cricketers hopping mad? (8)
24. A bully-off starts this game (6)
25. A transfer usually takes place at this price (6)
26. A type of bowling to make you dizzy? (8)

CLUES DOWN

1. Played on a diamond (8)
2. Neither too short nor too long a race? (6,8)
3. Clubs hope for a record one to bring in the money (10)
4. Not from 7 across, but very close (6)
5. A sad sportsman from university? (4)
6. Steve played soccer for Millwall and Wales (6)
9. There's plenty of shunts and dunts in this kind of motor sport (5,3,6)
14. Big Peter plays most of his golf in America these days (10)
17. You won't get far doing this without a paddle (8)
19. What wrestlers have had when they submit (6)
20. A helping hand to score a goal in ice-hockey (6)
23. What footballers change at half-time (4)

ANSWERS ON PAGE 49

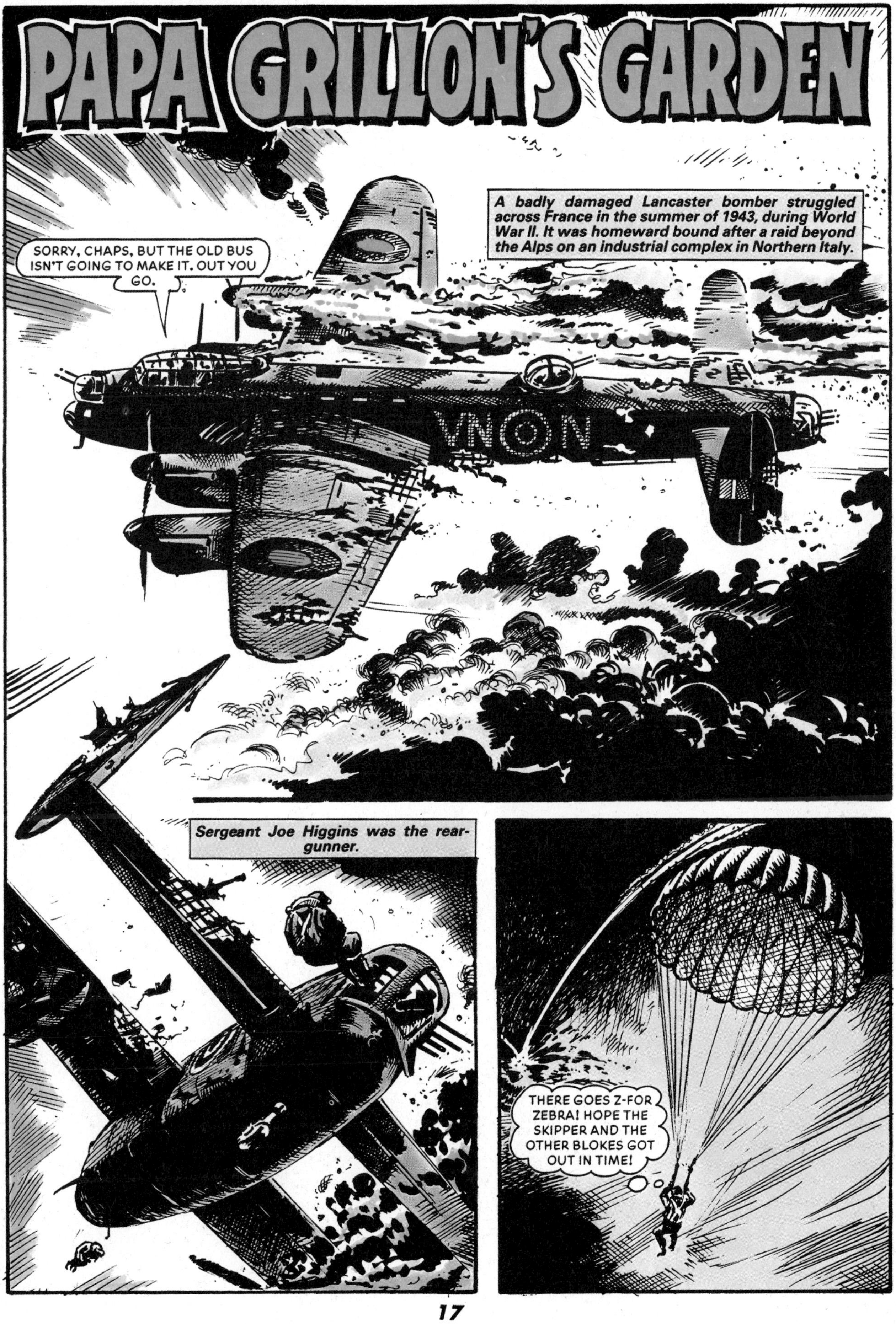
PAPA GRILLON'S GARDEN
A badly damaged Lancaster bomber struggled across France in the summer of 1943, during World War II. It was homeward bound after a raid beyond the Alps on an industrial complex in Northern Italy.
SORRY, CHAPS, BUT THE OLD BUS ISN'T GOING TO MAKE IT. OUT YOU GO.
VN O N
Sergeant Joe Higgins was the rear-gunner.
THERE GOES Z-FOR ZEBRA! HOPE THE SKIPPER AND THE OTHER BLOKES GOT OUT IN TIME!

The ground came up to meet Joe, when suddenly —
STREWTH! I'M STUCK!
ACHTUNG!
AHH! I'M HIT!
TRUST ME TO LAND IN BLOOMING NETTLES!
RAF — GOOD! COME! YOU MUST HURRY.
HUH! A LITTLE FROG IN A NIGHTSHIRT.
TOO BAD YOU FALL AMONG THE FEW ROSES I HAVE LEFT TO TEND. MUCH BETTER YOU HAD INFLICTED DAMAGE ON THE FOODSTUFFS I AM COMPELLED TO GROW FOR THE BOCHE!
SO IT WASN'T NETTLES, BUT A BED OF ROSES!

IT'S A BLINKING CASTLE!
CHATEAU LA TERRE, A PLACE OF HISTORY NOW SHAMED BY BEING HEADQUARTERS FOR SS ARMOURED DIVISION HEIMDALL — AND YOU, MY FRIEND, HAVE LANDED INSIDE ITS GREAT WALLS!
A SECRET WAY ONCE USED BY THE LORDS OF LA TERRE FOR PRIVATE BUSINESS OUTSIDE THE CHATEAU. THE ROOF LONG AGO FELL IN, BUT IT WILL MAKE YOU A SAFE HIDING PLACE.
Joe followed the steps of long-dead lords . . .
LET YOUR PARACHUTE BE A BED TILL I COME AGAIN. I AM PAUL GRILLON, BUT USUALLY KNOWN AS PAPA.
JOE HIGGINS, PAPA — AND THANKS!
WHAT A BLOOMING HOLE. I SUPPOSE I'D BETTER SETTLE IN AND DO SOMETHING ABOUT THIS SCRATCH IN MY SIDE.
Papa Grillon returned at dawn —
THIS WOUND IS NOTHING. I SUFFERED THREE MUCH WORSE IN THE BIG WAR.
IT WON'T STOP ME TRAVELLING. PAPA, HOW DO I GET OUT OF HERE?
JOE, THE WALLS OF LA TERRE ARE NOT EASY TO PASS. I AM ALLOWED OUT TO VISIT MY SON MARCEL, WHO IS A BAKER IN THE VILLAGE. MARCEL IS WITH THE RESISTANCE AND MAY BE ABLE TO HELP.
ENJOY THE ROSES I BRING FROM MY GARDEN, JOE — HAVE PATIENCE. FROM THE BOCHE I HEAR THAT YOU ARE THE ONLY ONE OF YOUR CREW STILL AT LIBERTY!

Joe settled to waiting —
THE ROOF MAY BE DOWN, BUT THERE'S STILL AIR COMING ALONG THIS SECRET WAY OF THE LORDS.
ALLO
PAPA WITH MY DAILY RATION OF BREAD, CHEESE, COFFEE AND ANOTHER BUNCH OF HIS BLOOMING ROSES. THE OLD BOY NEVER MISSES.
THE WOUND HEALS WELL, JOE. SOON YOU MAY BE TRAVELLING. MY SON MARCEL HAS A PLAN TO SMUGGLE YOU OUT ON THE COAL WAGON AFTER THE NEXT DELIVERY TO THE CHATEAU.
THAT SOUNDS MUCKY, BUT PROMISING.
Papa Grillon suddenly stopped coming —
THREE DAYS WITHOUT A VISIT. SOMETHING'S WRONG.
THAT MUST BE PAPA'S HOUSE. NO SMOKE — LOOKS EMPTY.
JUST A BIT OF MOULDY BREAD. NO SIGN OF THE OLD MAN.
JERRIES!

AGAINST THE WALL WITH HIM.
PAPA, YOUR LAST CHANCE TO TELL HOW THIS BIT OF NYLON FROM A PARACHUTE CAME TO BE SNAGGED ON ONE OF YOUR ROSE BUSHES.
PERHAPS IT BLEW IN ON THE WIND — AS YOU BOCHE ONE DAY WILL BE BLOWN OUT OF FRANCE.
THEY CAN'T MEAN TO SHOOT THE OLD MAN! IT ISN'T POSSIBLE.
SHOOT!
Later, back in the secret place —
IT'S UP TO ME . . . I'VE GOT TO MAKE MY OWN WAY OUT.
THIS MUST BE THE BASE OF THE OUTER WALL. TWENTY FEET THICK, OLD PAPA SAID.
FRESH AIR — DAYLIGHT. I'VE MADE IT!

THE VILLAGE! I'D BETTER WAIT TILL DARK BEFORE SLIPPING IN FOR A VISIT TO PAPA'S SON, THE BAKER.
England, one month later —
LOOK, SIR, ISN'T ANYBODY INTERESTED IN ME KNOWING A WAY INTO THE HEADQUARTERS OF A JERRY ARMOURED DIVISION?
I'M SURE SOMEBODY WILL BE, SERGEANT. WHY DON'T YOU SUBMIT A NICE CLEAR REPORT, THEN GO OFF AND ENJOY YOUR REPATRIATION LEAVE?
NO, SIR — NO REPORT. I MEAN TO BE IN ON ANY USE MADE OF WHAT I KNOW.
OBSTINATE YOUNG FELLOW.
SS ARMOURED DIVISION HEIMDALL, THE BUTCHERS OF THE UKRAINE! TEMPTING, BY JOVE! OLD CHAP, DO YOU MIND IF I BORROW SERGEANT HIGGINS?
HELP YOURSELF, OLD BOY.
Joe found his leave replaced by a very special course —
HUP! HUP! KEEP THEM SOGGY LEGS MOVING!
TRY TO LAND ON YOUR FEET, SON!

Evening, after a punishing ten days —
SERGEANT HIGGINS, MEET SMALL SCALE RAIDING FORCE SIX. WE RATHER HOPE YOU WILL VOLUNTEER TO HELP US WITH A LITTLE JOB.
CHATEAU LA TERRE! YOU MAY BACK OUT NOW IF YOU WISH, SERGEANT.
NO, SIR. I'M NOT BACKING OUT.
Three nights later —
OUR DIVERSION RAID'S DRAWING JERRY FLAK.
ON YOUR WAY, LADS.
Joe drifted down again over hostile country —
RESISTANCE BEACON FIRES! THIS IS A BIT DIFFERENT TO THE LAST TIME.
SIR, THIS IS MARCEL GRILLON. HE HELPED ME GET BACK TO BLIGHTY ALONG THE LIFELINE ROUTE.
NOW I WELCOME YOU BACK AND WISH YOU LUCK. HIT THEM HARD, JOE.

The raiders slipped through the night —
THERE'S ARMOUR LAAGERED ALL ROUND THIS AREA, SIR.
THE CHINESE HAVE A SAYING, JOE — CRACK SKULL OF DRAGON AND THE BODY DIES.
BLIMEY! THAT DUMP IS BLOOMING BIG.
ISN'T IT JUST. FOLLOW JOE HIGGINS, LADS.
IT'S A BIT TIGHT ALONG THIS STRETCH. KEEP YOUR HEADS DOWN.
TEAMS FORM UP. FIRST JOB IS THE SENTRIES ON THE MAIN GATE AND DUNGEON DOORS.

ON YOUR MARKS, MY TEAM! LET'S GO!
THE BUTCHERS AT MESS. GIVE 'EM THEIR AFTERS, JOE.
NOW THE WAR-ROOM, JOE. MIGHT FIND SOME USEFUL PAPER.
Joe sighted a familiar face —
ACH! WER IST DA?
MAJOR, THIS COVE'S MINE.
THIS IS FOR PAPA GRILLON.

Another raiding team dealt with the causeway —
TANKS COMING FROM THE PARK.
GOOD-OH! WE'LL INCLUDE A COUPLE IN THE BLOW-UP.
THE MAJOR'S BLOWING 'END OF GAME.'
LOOKS LIKE THE LADS HAVE BEEN CARELESS WITH MATCHES.
The raiders mustered at the sundial entrance to the secret way —
DOG PEPPER, SIR! BACKTRACKS WELL DOSED IN CASE JERRY PUTS MUTTS ON OUR SCENT.
HURRY IT UP. WHERE THE BLAZES IS JOE HIGGINS?
HERE I AM, SIR. I HAD TO PICK A BUNCH OF ROSES.
YOU WHAT? OH, ALL RIGHT — COME ON.
RELAX NOW, CHAPS. WE HOLE UP HERE TILL THE HEAT IS REDUCED TO A MILD GLOW, THEN WE MAKE OUR WAY TO THAT SECRET RESISTANCE AIRSTRIP IN THE COMPIEGNE FOREST.
The village churchyard two days later —
YOU MAKE A VISIT TO THE GRAVE OF YOUR FATHER, MARCEL.
YES, JEAN. I TAKE HIM A FEW ROSES PICKED BY A FRIEND!
THE END

THE SWORD OF THE SHENSI

COULD NOT ALL THE WEALTH OF THE OKADA PURCHASE BETTER SWORDS THAN THESE? SEE — I WILL SHOW YOU WHAT A REAL BLADE WILL DO!
BITE DEEP, SWORD OF THE SHENSI!
AARGH!
HE IS LIKE A HERO OUT OF ANCIENT TIMES. NONE CAN STAND AGAINST HIM!
TELL YOUR FATHER THE SAME TREATMENT AWAITS HIM TOO, IF EVER WE SHOULD MEET!
FLEE!
And so . . .
HE DEFEATED US, FATHER. HE IS THE DEADLIEST FIGHTER WE HAVE EVER SEEN.
FOOLS! THERE ARE MORE WAYS THAN ONE OF SILENCING AN ENEMY! WE HAVE TRIED STEEL AND FAILED. SO, LET US NOW TRY HONEY!
SEND WORD TO HIM THAT IT IS TIME THIS FEUD CEASED. SAY THAT IF HE WILL COME TO THIS HOUSE AS OUR GUEST WE WILL DISCUSS OUR DIFFERENCES IN FRIENDSHIP AND SETTLE THEM. AND NEVER FEAR, MY SONS — FOR HE WILL COME!
Joji Okada was right, for Saburo knew that by the ancient laws of hospitality he was as safe in his enemy's house as he was in his own . . .
WELCOME, SABURO SHENSI. YOU DO THIS HOUSE GREAT HONOUR.
Later . . .
A TRULY MAGNIFICENT MEAL. AND NOW SHALL WE DISCUSS HOW WE CAN BEST PUT AN END TO THIS MOST UNNECESSARY FEUD?
BUT OF COURSE. WE OF THE OKADA HAVE COME TO A DECISION. WE THINK THAT THE ONE THING THAT WILL BRING PEACE BETWEEN OUR TWO FAMILIES . . .

. . . IS YOUR DEATH!
TREACHERY? BUT . . . BUT . . . THE SACRED LAWS OF HOSPITALITY — YOU WOULD NEVER AFFRONT THE GODS BY VIOLATING THEM!
AAGH!
FOOL! DO YOU NOT REALISE THAT THE GREAT AND POWERFUL OKADA ARE ABOVE ALL LAWS?
JOJI OKADA — FOR THIS DAY'S WORK A CURSE WILL LIE FOREVER ON YOU AND YOUR DESCENDANTS. IF EVER MY SWORD IS HELD BY SOMEONE IN THE PRESENCE OF AN OKADA, THEN MY SPIRIT WILL ENTER THAT ONE. AND THEN SHALL HE CRY, "BITE DEEP, SWORD OF THE SHENSI!" AND THE OKADA'S LIFE BLOOD WILL SPILL!
AND SO HE DIES — WITH TALES TO FRIGHTEN CHILDREN STILL ON HIS LIPS. FETCH HIS SWORD TO ME. I WISH TO SEE MORE CLOSELY WHAT WILL BE THE "TERROR" OF THE OKADA!
MY LORD OKADA!

BITE DEEP, SWORD OF THE SHENS!!
ARCHERS — CUT HIM DOWN!
Too late . . .
FATHER! FATHER!
NO, HE IS DEAD — SLAIN BY THE SWORD, JUST AS THE MAN WE MURDERED SAID. BROTHER, WE ARE ACCURSED!
The brothers could think of only one way of lifting the curse . . .
INTO THE SEA WITH IT.
AND THERE LET IT REMAIN TO THE END OF TIME — WHERE IT WILL TROUBLE US NO MORE.
But some days later a poor fisherman called Musiro found something caught in his net . . .
A SAMURAI SWORD! I HAVE NEVER SEEN ANYTHING MORE BEAUTIFUL! IT SHALL BE GIVEN A PLACE OF HONOUR IN MY HOUSE — AND SHALL BE HANDED DOWN FROM FATHER TO SON OF THE MUSIROS FOR EVER.
Hundreds of years later, in 1945, at a Japanese prisoner-of-war camp in Burma of which the latest Okada was Commandant . . .
THE EXECUTIONER HAS ARRIVED, MAJOR OKADA, AND ALL IS NOW READY. BUT IS IT WISE TO GO THROUGH WITH THIS? THE PUNISHMENT FOR A PRISONER ATTEMPTING TO ESCAPE IS INDEED DEATH BUT, SIR — WE ALL KNOW THAT OUR COUNTRY WILL BE SURRENDERING TO THE ALLIES WITHIN HOURS, AND —
LIEUTENANT, IF THE MAN HAD TRIED TO ESCAPE ONLY FIVE MINUTES BEFORE THE TREATY WAS SIGNED, MY DECISION WOULD STILL REMAIN THE SAME. COME, LET US SEE THE PUNISHMENT CARRIED OUT.
IT'S MURDER, THAT'S WHAT IT IS — MURDER! THE JAPS ARE PRACTICALLY DEFEATED, AND THEY'RE STILL BEHAVING LIKE ANIMALS.
IF ONLY THOSE GUARDS WOULD TAKE THEIR EYES OFF US FOR A MINUTE, WE COULD JUMP 'EM, FREE BERT AND HOLD THE CAMP TILL THE SURRENDER. BUT WE'RE ONLY DREAMING, MATE — BERT'S FOR THE CHOP, AND THERE'S NOTHING WE CAN DO ABOUT IT.

SERGEANT MUSIRO, SIR — EXECUTIONER.
THAT SWORD — IT IS MAGNIFICENT. WHERE DID YOU GET IT?
FROM MY FATHER, SIR — AND HIS FATHER BEFORE HIM, AND SO BACK INTO THE MISTS OF TIME. NO-ONE NOW KNOWS HOW IT FIRST CAME INTO OUR FAMILY.
I SEE. SERGEANT — I HAVE DECIDED THAT I WISH TO TRY THIS FINE SWORD. AND SO I WILL EXECUTE THE PRISONER, MYSELF.
AND SO LET JAPANESE JUSTICE BE CARRIED OUT!
THE RAT — HE'S ENJOYING IT. YOU KNOW, IF EVER THERE WAS A BLOKE I'D WILLINGLY SWING FOR, IT'S OKADA.
But then . . .
THE . . . THE SWORD! IT IS TWISTING IN MY HANDS!
BITE DEEP, SWORD OF THE SHENSI! AAAAGH!
BLIMEY — HE'S COMMITTED SUICIDE!
AND ALL THE JAP GUARDS HAVE TURNED TO WATCH. COME ON, BOYS — THIS IS OUR BIG CHANCE!
TAKE THAT, YOU MURDERING SWINE!
URRRRH!
Soon it was all over . . .
WHY DID HE DO IT?
THAT WE'LL NEVER KNOW. BUT ONE THING'S FOR SURE, MATE — HE CERTAINLY GOT WHAT HE DESERVED!
THE END.

THE LAMBTON WORM
AND OTHER LEGENDS OF LONG AGO

The reason there are no snakes in Ireland today is said to be that Saint Patrick drove them into a deep pool in the Kerry Hills, where they drowned.

The Lambton Worm was a fierce monster which terrorised the district of Lambton, in Durham. A witch told a young squire how to kill the Worm, but made him promise to slay the first living thing he saw afterwards — which turned out to be his own father. The squire broke his promise, and a curse lay on his family for nine generations.

When any thirsty man stood on a magic mound in the ancient forest of Gloucestershire, a cup-bearer with a drinking horn would appear. One knight who drank there stole the horn, and was put to death for his crime by the Earl of Gloucester.

Finding a cask in a highland cave, Donald McKay bored a hole in it and a tiny figure popped out. It began to grow and grow and Donald was scared stiff. The figure, now gigantic, asked Donald if he was amazed. "I would be even more amazed if you could become tiny enough to enter the cask again," said Donald. The figure did so — and Donald plugged the cask!

At sunrise on May-day each year, the figure of an ancient Irish chieftain, O'Donoghue, appears from the waters of Lake Killarney. As he rides across the lake mysterious music is heard. It stops when the chieftain disappears back into the depths.

A cobbler, going home from Shrewsbury with a sack of shoes for repair, met a giant on his way to dam the River Severn with a huge spadeful of earth, so flooding the town. The cobbler said he had worn out all the shoes walking from far-off Shrewsbury. The giant, in despair, dumped the earth, forming the hill now called the Wrekin.

Walking near his home town of Richmond, in Yorkshire, Peter Thomson came across a secret cave. Inside lay King Arthur and the Knights of the Round Table, fast asleep. When Peter tried to draw the King's sword from its scabbard hanging on the wall, the sleepers began to waken. In a panic, Peter replaced the sword and they went back to sleep. Peter fled, and it is said Arthur and his knights still slumber in the cave.

Fishermen at Orford, in Suffolk, caught a merman in the 13th century. For six months he was kept alive in a rock-bound pool, fed on raw fish. Then, growing tired of captivity, the merman escaped back to the open sea.

Death of a King
In August 1100 AD, as England lay under the harsh rule of William Rufus, a secret meeting of Norman nobles took place near the city of Winchester . . .
SO WE ARE AGREED? WE ARE FOR HENRY AND RUFUS MUST DIE.
AYE!
EACH OF YOU TAKE A PEBBLE FROM THE HELMET OFFERED BY MY MAN AP EVAN. HE WHO PLUCKS THE BLACK PEBBLE IS THE ONE CHOSEN FOR THE DEED. YET HE MUST NOT ANNOUNCE HIMSELF, BUT SHALL KEEP THIS CHOOSING SECRET.
WHY THIS SECRECY, DE MAHAUD? WHY SHOULD WE NOT ALL KNOW WHO IS TO SLAY THE DOG?
NOT KNOWING BINDS US ALL TO WHAT IS DONE, DE BRACY. NONE OF US WILL BE ABLE TO POINT AND SAY — IT WAS HE WHO STRUCK THE BLOW.
Shortly . . .
BROTHER HUGO, WHO THINK YOU TOOK THE BLACK PEBBLE?
THERE WAS NO BLACK PEBBLE. THIS KILLING OF THE KING I TRUST ONLY TO MYSELF.

IT SHALL BE DONE ON THE CHASE, BROTHER ODO — AS THE RED KING HUNTS HIS RED DEER. WALTER TIREL, AS EVER, WILL BE AT HIS STIRRUP. A POOR SPORTSMAN IS WALTER WITH HIS FONDNESS FOR THE BOW INSTEAD OF THE LANCE.
A SHORT HORSE-BOW, BROTHER — A PUNY WEAPON WHEN COMPARED WITH THE STURDY WELSH BOW OF AP EVAN.
A few days later, King William Rufus hunted with his nobles . . .
YOU OUTRIDE ALL AS ALWAYS, MY LIEGE.
FORGET THOSE SLUGGARDS, WAT TIREL. PRESS ON.
HOLD HARD! WAIT!
WHAT IS IT, DE MAHAUD?
MY LORDS, I KNOW THIS GROUND. FOLLOW ME AND WE'LL CUT A CORNER ON THE KING.
COME! FOR ONCE WE COULD BEAT RUFUS TO THE KILL.

The stag was brought to bay . . .
THE HOUNDS HAVE HIM, WAT.
Suddenly . . .
AARGH!
MY LIEGE!
The hunt caught up . . .
THE KING IS DEAD!
SO WE SEE, WALTER TIREL. SPIKED BY AN ARROW AND YOU WITH BOW IN HAND.
IT WAS NOT I. NOT A SHAFT HAS LEFT MY BOW THIS DAY.
LET US TRUST YOU WILL BE STILL SAYING SO AFTER A TOUCH OF THE HOT IRONS.
NO! NO! I'LL NOT WAIT FOR THAT!

LET HIM FLEE. HE WILL FIND NO SANCTUARY AND OUR DUTY IS TO OUR DEAD KING!
ESCORT HIM TO WINCHESTER WITH THE DIGNITY THAT IS DUE. MEANWHILE MY BROTHER AND I WILL RIDE ON TO BREAK THIS DIRE NEWS TO PRINCE HENRY.
BROTHER HUGO, THINK YOU ENGLAND WILL BE BETTER FOR WHAT WE HAVE DONE?
LITTLE BROTHER, IT CERTAINLY SHOULD BE FOR US BARONS WITHOUT THE IRON HAND OF RUFUS ON OUR NECKS.
A FINE SHOT, AP EVAN. DID YOU HIDE YOUR WELSH BOW AS I BADE YOU?
AYE, MASTER. THAT YEW STICK IS WHERE IT WILL NOT BE FOUND.
YOU DID WELL, AP EVAN.
URGH!
A LESSON FOR YOU, BROTHER. TAKE NO CHANCES ON A SERVANT WHO HAS LEARNED TOO MUCH!
A short while later . . .
GOOD HUGO, IS IT DONE? MAY I NOW SEIZE THE TREASURY AND HAVE MYSELF ACCLAIMED BY THE BARONS?
YOUR HIGHNESS, THE KING IS DEAD! LONG LIVE THE KING!

HIGHNESS, I WOULD BE THE FIRST TO PLEDGE YOU THE FEALTY OF MY HOUSE.
NAY, HUGO — ARISE. THIS IS NOT THE TIME.
BESIDES, YOU MADE THE SAME PLEDGE TO MY POOR MURDERED BROTHER. HUGO, YOU HAVE SERVED ME WELL, BUT HOW CAN I PUT TRUST IN ONE WHO WOULD SLAY HIS KING?
BUT, MY LIEGE . . .
AARGH!
NO! NO! AARGH!
THIS NEW KING . . . SEEMS TO KNOW THE LESSON YOU WERE TEACHING ME, HUGO!
TRUE, BROTHER . . . URRH . . . HE SHOULD DO WELL.
The End

FIGARO!
THESE INDIANS SURE HAVE FUNNY CUSTOMS!
INDIAN CUSTOMS
WAR PAINT! THAT GIVES ME AN IDEA FOR ROBBING THE BANK!
APPLYING WAR PAINT
THE BANK-MAN WILL BE SO SCARED WHEN HE SEES MY PAINTED FACE, THAT HE'LL GIVE ME ALL THE MONEY!
IN TOWN...
YAHOO! IT'S FIERCE, FRIGHTENING FIGARO!
BANK
HELLO, FIGARO...
...UP TO YOUR USUAL TRICKS, EH?
AREN'T YOU SCARED OF MY PAINTED FACE?
PAINTED FA-? OH, I DIDN'T NOTICE!
LOOK AT FIGARO'S FACE, LADS! FUNNY, EH?
HO! HO! HO!
PAH! WAR PAINT ISN'T FRIGHTENING ENOUGH!
BANK
BACK AT THE SHACK...
WHAT ELSE IS IN THIS BOOK?
GOSH! SOME SORT OF INDIAN MASK! THAT'S FRIGHTENING! I'LL MAKE ONE!
INDIAN LEGEND SAYS THAT ONE DAY THIS SPIRIT WILL APPEAR AND BRING RICHES TO ALL THE TRIBES.
OH-OH! FIGARO DIDN'T READ THIS, READERS!
LATER...
THERE! THIS'LL SCARE THOSE BANK FOLK!
CREEP IN QUIETLY, THEN...
AWOO!
EEK!
YIPPEE! SUCCESS!
OOH! IT WAS TERRIBLE! TERRIBLE!
I'M RICH... AFTER ALL THESE YEARS!
IT UM SPIRIT WITH UM RICHES... JUST LIKE UM LEGEND SAYS!
STOP, HEAP SPIRIT! GIVE US UM RICHES!
WAHOO! UM TRIBE HEAP WEALTHY!
HELP!
MIDNIGHT... AND FIGARO'S GANG ARRIVE...
JUMP, FAILURE, BEFORE WE CHANGE OUR MINDS!

AN IRON CROSS FOR KRANTZ
COME ON, OTTO. SHOW THIS CHEEKY NEW KID A THING OR TWO.
Otto Krantz and Bruno Kahn were rivals from way back before World War II. Their first meeting was at school in Germany and was to set the pattern for a rivalry that became a running battle ever after.
I MAY BE NEW BUT I'M NOT GOING TO BE PUSHED ABOUT BY ANY FAT IDIOT LIKE YOU!
Later, on the sports field—
IF YOU PAIR CAN CEASE EXCHANGING INSULTS LONG ENOUGH, WE CAN GET ON WITH THE RACE.
THAT FAT CHUMP THINKS HE HAS A CHANCE AGAINST ME. TALK ABOUT THE TORTOISE AND THE HARE!
ONCE THROUGH THE WOOD AND I'M ALMOST HOME. FANCY 'CORPULENT' KRANTZ MANAGING TO KEEP UP.
I'M NEARLY WHACKED, BUT THAT ROTTER LOOKS AS IF HE COULD RUN ALL DAY.
ONE LAST EFFORT, BUT FIRST TO GET RID OF KAHN.
HEY! WATCH WHAT YOU ARE DOING, YOU DOLT.

NO TIME FOR A BATHE, KAHN, BUT IT MIGHT COOL YOUR ENTHUSIASM DOWN.
YOU LOUSY CHEAT! YOU PUSHED ME DELIBERATELY!
And so—
YOU PUSHED ME INTO THE RIVER. YOU KNEW I WOULD HAVE WON IF YOU HADN'T CHEATED.
COME NOW, KAHN. DON'T BE SUCH A BAD SPORT. I'M SURE OTTO WOULD NEVER HAVE DONE SUCH A THING. YOU SLIPPED AND THAT'S THAT.
A few years later—
OF ALL THE ROTTEN LUCK. I JOIN THE ARMY AND FIND THAT KRANTZ IS HERE. IN THE SAME CLASS TOO.
THOUGHT I'D SEEN THE LAST OF KAHN WHEN I LEFT SCHOOL. HE'D BETTER NOT GET IN MY WAY OR I'LL FIX HIM GOOD.
CONGRATULATIONS, CADET KAHN. TOP OF YOUR CLASS FOR THE YEAR 1938, THOUGH CADET KRANTZ CAME A VERY CLOSE SECOND.
CURSE KAHN! BUT FOR HIM I'D BE TOP CADET!
Later—
I GOT RIGHT-THROUGH GREEN FORCE'S SENTRIES. AND YOU WOULD THINK THOSE TWO WERE ON A PICNIC AND NOT THE PASSING OUT WAR GAMES.
OLD FAT KRANTZ IS ONE OF THE RED FORCE RAIDING COMMANDOS. BUT I DOUBT IF HE COULD SNEAK THROUGH THE LINES.
BOMBEN
DID IT! YOU PAIR OF CHUMPS NEVER GOT THE CHANCE TO FIRE BLANKS. NEVER SAW ME SNEAKING UP.
BOMBEN
HIMMEL! ACCORDING TO THE RULES THIS BRIDGE IS BLOWN. WE REALLY WILL BE FOR IT NOW. THE COLONEL WILL JUMP ON US FEET FIRST.

WHAT A NEAR THING THAT WAS. BUT I SAW THE GUARDS KNEW OF YOUR APPROACH AND COULD HAVE SHOT YOU DOWN BEFORE YOU REACHED THE BRIDGE.
YOU LIE! AN UMPIRE IS SUPPOSED TO BE NEUTRAL!
In 1939 war came, and with it a string of victories for the Wehrmacht.
JUST MY LUCK. THE SECOND BATTALION STUCK HERE IN THE FATHERLAND AND OTHER FELLOWS GETTING ALL THE GLORY.
ALL YOU TALK ABOUT IS WINNING AN IRON CROSS, KRANTZ!
1941—
LET ME INTRODUCE OUR NEW FELLOW. MAJOR KAHN WAS SERVING WITH THE FIRST BATTALION BUT IS NOW WITH US. QUITE AN ASSET, EH, KRANTZ?
KAHN! NOT ONLY A MAJOR BUT HE HAS THE IRON CROSS. TRULY THE DEVIL MUST LOOK AFTER HIS OWN.
ACTION COMING AT LAST. WE ARE TO HAVE A GO AT THE RUSSKIES.
AND HERE'S TO MY IRON CROSS. I SHALL FIND IT IN RUSSIA.
And so—
THESE RUSSIANS ARE NOT SO TOUGH. WE REALLY HAVE THEM ON THE RUN NOW. IVAN IS FINISHED. CRUSHED BY THE MIGHT AND COURAGE OF THE WEHRMACHT.
HOPE HE FINDS SOME FIGHT SOON. OTHERWISE MY IRON CROSS WILL REMAIN JUST A DREAM.
Later—
GET THAT BLASTED DOOR SHUT. DO YOU WANT ME TO FREEZE TO DEATH?
THE NEW MAJOR HAS ARRIVED, SIR. LOOKS A BIT OF A MEAN CUSS TO ME. HE'S WITH THE OLD MAN NOW. WANTS YOU TO CUT OVER THERE.
AH, CAPTAIN. MAJOR KAHN IS TAKING OVER YOUR COMPANY NOW. HE WILL REPLACE MAJOR FROLICH WHO STEPPED ON THE MINE LAST WEEK.
KAHN! I THOUGHT HE WAS WITH THE B. COMPANY STAFF. I SHALL HAVE TO WATCH MY STEP HERE.

I HAVE A JOB FOR AN IRON CROSS CANDIDATE, KRANTZ. JUST UP YOUR STREET. TAKE A DETAIL AND OCCUPY HILL FIVE UNTIL FURTHER ORDERS.
THAT HEAP OF DIRT IS WELL IN FRONT OF OUR FORWARD POSITIONS. AND WITH A RUSSIAN ATTACK IMMINENT IT IS A SUICIDE JOB. HE WANTS ME TO GET THE CHOP.
Soon—
WE HAVE TO PULL BACK. I CAN'T HOLD HERE!
YOU WILL HAVE TO HOLD THEM, KRANTZ. WE NEED TIME HERE. I'M SURE YOU CAN DO IT.
THE LOUSY SKUNK WANTS ME TO DIE OUT HERE ON A LIMB. HE'S JUST HOPING WE GET WIPED OUT AND WON'T LIFT A FINGER TO HELP US.
RIGHT! I'M NOT GOING TO DIE. AND WE ARE GOING TO THROW THESE IVANS RIGHT OFF OUR HILL. FOLLOW ME, MEN. LET'S GET STUCK IN.
KRANTZ IS A FIGHTING FOOL. THOSE RUSSKIES ARE RUNNING. LOOKS LIKE OUR GALLANT CAPTAIN WILL GET HIS CROSS FOR THIS BIT OF WORK.
Later—
HOLDING THE HILL AGAINST SUCH ODDS WAS QUITE A STUNT. SOME COMMANDING OFFICERS MIGHT DEEM IT WORTHY OF A DECORATION.
I DID WRITE A RECOMMENDATION YOU SHOULD BE DECORATED, KRANTZ, FOR ONE REASON. SO YOU COULD SEE WHERE I THINK IT BELONGS!
YOU DEVIL! YOU WOULDN'T PUT MY NAME FORWARD IF I TOOK STALINGRAD SINGLE HANDED.
OUR OFFENSIVE HAS FAILED! THE SIXTH ARMY IS DOOMED, AND YOU WITH IT. I HAVE A FRIEND WHO IS TO WANGLE ME ON AN AIRCRAFT TOMORROW. IT WILL BE THE LAST ONE TO LEAVE!
AND YOU WANT ME TO DIE WITH THE SIXTH. ROT OUT HERE WHILST YOU ARE SAFE BACK IN THE FATHERLAND.

Later—
MY ELECTRICAL FLAIR CAME IN HANDY. A NICE LITTLE DOLLY HERE TO SEND KAHN WHERE HE BELONGS.
I KNOW IT'S THE END OF THE ROAD, BUT WOULD YOU SEE MY NIECE GETS THIS? I SHALL NOT BE ALIVE TO SEE HER BIRTHDAY. YOU KNOW WHERE SHE LIVES, I KNOW.
ER, OF COURSE. I SHALL SEE SHE GETS IT, NEVER FEAR.
THE LEAST I CAN DO FOR THE POOR DEVIL. HE WILL BE EITHER DEAD OR A SIBERIA-BOUND PRISONER SOON.
But as Kahn's plane took off—
GOT HIM! BUT HE PUT A BURST INTO OUR PORT ENGINE. WE SHALL HAVE TO TURN BACK NOW.
DONNER WETTER! THEY HAVE RUN INTO TROUBLE. AND THAT BOMB IS DUE TO GO OFF ANY SECOND NOW.
THIS APPROACH IS GOING TO BE TRICKY. HOLD TIGHT THERE.
THAT CROSS IS COMING DOWN. I SHAN'T BE ABLE TO DODGE IT. ARGHHHHH!
POOR OLD KRANTZ! HE NEVER STOOD A CHANCE WITH THAT THING FALLING ON HIM.
HE ALWAYS WANTED AN IRON CROSS — AND HE GOT IT! ALL HALF A TON OF IT!
The End

The DRUMMER BOYS

FIRE GRAPE AND CAN ISTER SHOT!
THIS IS THEIR LAST BID TO PREVENT OUR GUNS FIRING AT THEIR COLUMNS CROSSING THE FROZEN RIVER. THEIR MARSHAL VICTOR HIMSELF COMMANDS THIS REARGUARD.
OUR COSSACK CAVALRY WILL HASTEN THEIR RETREAT!
FORM SQUARE! VOLLEY FIRE!
HURRAH! CHARGE!
FALL BACK TO THE RIVER BANK!
THE REMNANTS OF OUR MAIN FORCES ARE STILL CROSSING, MARSHAL.
BUT ONCE THOSE RUSSIAN GUNS GET INTO POSITION TO FIRE, THE ICE WILL BE BROKEN LIKE THAT BRIDGE, COLONEL.
I MUST REJOIN OUR ARMY NOW. LET THE WOUNDED AND DRUMMER LADS COME WITH ME. HOLD ON HERE WITH YOUR REGIMENT FOR A WHILE LONGER.

LET US STAY AND FIGHT WITH THE REGIMENT, COLONEL DANVERS!
YOU HEARD THE MARSHAL'S ORDERS! GET AWAY WITH THE WOUNDED!
MOVE ALONG NEAR THE BANK OUT OF THE COLONEL'S SIGHT!
WE CAN STILL GET BACK INTO THIS FIGHT BY CLIMBING UP THE HILL THROUGH THESE WOODS.
WE'RE BEHIND ENEMY POSITIONS NOW!
YES! THOSE GUNS ARE BEING MOVED TO FIRE AT OUR TROOPS STILL CROSSING THE RIVER.
OPEN FIRE TO DELAY THEM LIMBERING UP!

STOP SHOOTING NOW! FORM UP DOWN THIS HILL!
THE RUSSIANS MAY THINK OUR FIRING CAME FROM SHARP-SHOOTERS GOING AHEAD OF AN ATTACK. WHAT WILL THEY THINK WHEN THEY HEAR SO MANY DRUMS FROM BEHIND THIS HILL?
THAT WE LEAD AN ATTACK IN FORCE!
BEAT THE ADVANCE!
VIVE L'EMPEREUR!
LISTEN! FRENCH DRUMS!
THEY MUST HAVE SOMEHOW MOVED A FORCE AROUND TO OUR REAR! UNLIMBER THE GUNS!
SO MANY DRUMMERS! LEADING A REGIMENT AT LEAST! OPEN FIRE!

HALT HERE AS IF WAITING FOR THE REGIMENT TO FORM UP.
AAAH!
TAKE A TROOP OF YOUR COSSACKS UP THERE TO REPORT ON ENEMY STRENGTH!
CUT THEM DOWN!
NO! WAIT! THERE IS NOTHING BEHIND THEM!
A while later —
THE LAST OF OUR TROOPS HAVE GOT AWAY ACROSS THE ICE!
OUR COMMANDER, MARSHAL RAKOVSKI, WILL PROBABLY HAVE YOU LADS SHOT RATHER THAN KEEP YOU PRISONERS!
A CLEVER TRICK AND BRAVELY DONE! YOU SAVED YOUR COMRADES BY DELAYING OUR GUNS. TAKE ONE OF YOUR CAPTURED STANDARDS BACK AS A TOKEN OF OUR ADMIRATION!
THANK YOU, MARSHAL RAKOVSKI!
WE CAN BEAT RETREAT NOW, PIERRE!
YES, BUT WITH HONOUR! VIVE LA REGIMENT! VIVE L'EMPEREUR!
THE END

ANSWERS TO SPORTS CROSSWORD

	B		M		A		I		B				L	
P	A	K	I	S	T	A	N		L	I	S	T	O	N
	S		D		T		D		U		T		V	
N	E	E	D	L	E		I	C	E	D	O	V	E	R
	B		L		N		A				C		L	
P	A	T	E		D	O	N	C	O	C	K	E	L	L
	L		D		A				O		C			
A	L	B	I	O	N				S	N	A	T	C	H
			S		C				T		R		A	
G	E	N	T	L	E	P	A	C	E		R	I	N	K
	N		A				S		R		A		O	
B	O	U	N	C	E	R	S		H	O	C	K	E	Y
	U		C		N		I		U		I		I	
A	G	R	E	E	D		S	P	I	N	N	I	N	G
	H				S		T		S		G		G	

MORGYN THE MIGHTY
Morgyn the Mighty, the world's strongest man, was helping an old friend, Abu Dhur, and his son Ali, fish for pearls in the Persian Gulf.
Ali stayed under for 90 seconds. Then he returned with his haul—
FATHER, LOOK! A MAGNIFICENT PEARL!
IT'S A BEAUTY, ALI.
EVIL! WE DO NOT WANT ANYTHING SO VALUABLE!
WAIT, ABU!
HAVE SO MANY YEARS UNDERWATER ADDLED YOUR BRAINS, OLD FRIEND? WHY COMMIT SUCH A SENSELESS ACT?
NOT SENSELESS. SUCH LARGE PEARLS HAVE BEEN FOUND RECENTLY, BUT THEIR OWNERS HAVE BEEN MURDERED AND THE PEARLS STOLEN!
I UNDERSTAND YOUR FEARS, ABU. I SHALL KEEP THE PEARL FOR YOU UNTIL WE CAN TAKE IT TO THE CITY.
NAY! I CANNOT HAVE YOU TAKE A RISK. I SHALL SLEEP WITH IT UNDER MY PILLOW.

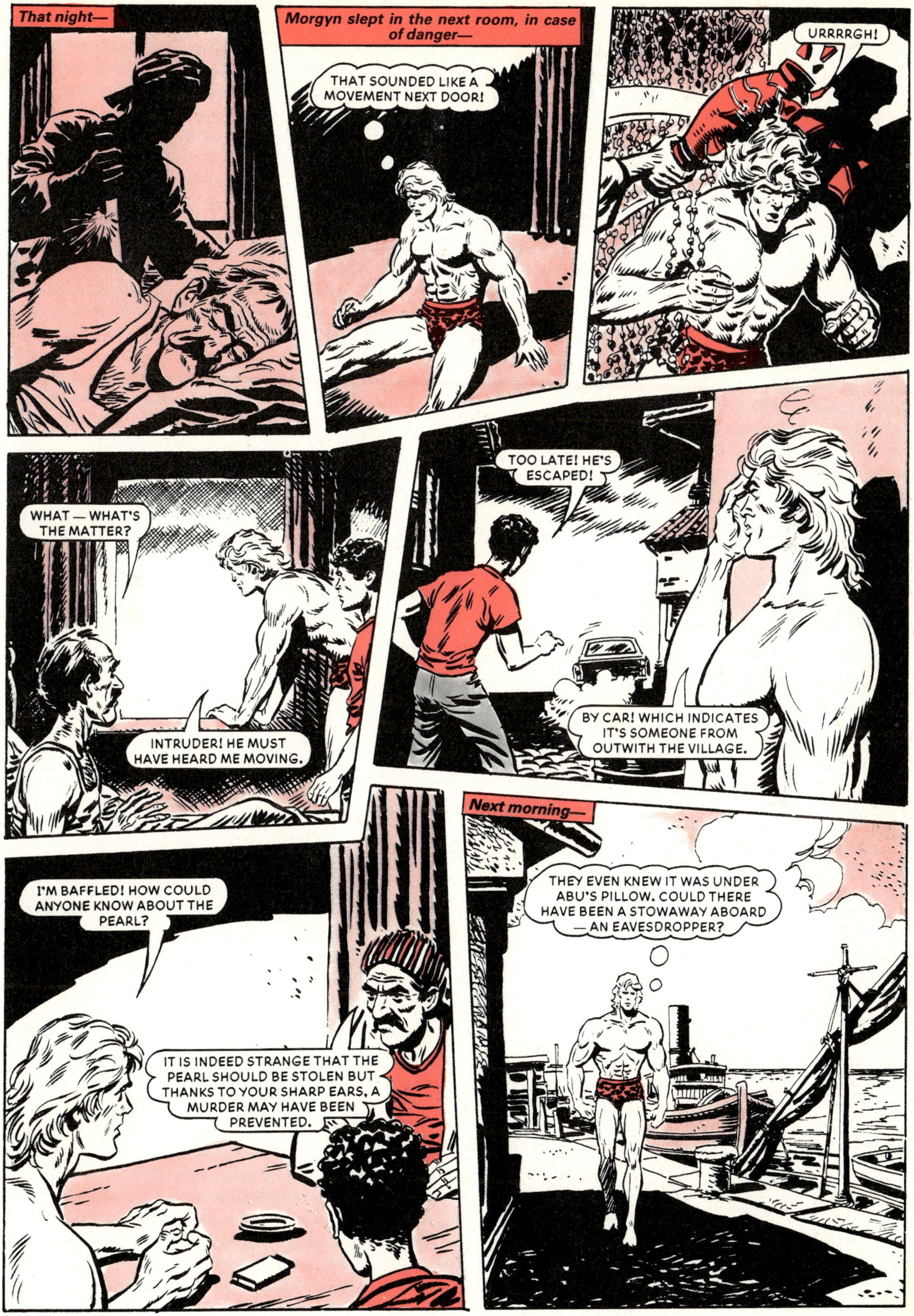
That night—
Morgyn slept in the next room, in case of danger—
THAT SOUNDED LIKE A MOVEMENT NEXT DOOR!
URRRRGH!
WHAT — WHAT'S THE MATTER?
INTRUDER! HE MUST HAVE HEARD ME MOVING.
TOO LATE! HE'S ESCAPED!
BY CAR! WHICH INDICATES IT'S SOMEONE FROM OUTWITH THE VILLAGE.
I'M BAFFLED! HOW COULD ANYONE KNOW ABOUT THE PEARL?
IT IS INDEED STRANGE THAT THE PEARL SHOULD BE STOLEN BUT THANKS TO YOUR SHARP EARS, A MURDER MAY HAVE BEEN PREVENTED.
Next morning—
THEY EVEN KNEW IT WAS UNDER ABU'S PILLOW. COULD THERE HAVE BEEN A STOWAWAY ABOARD — AN EAVESDROPPER?

Morgyn searched the dhow—
A HIGH-POWERED BUGGING DEVICE!
Every one of the village boats had a bug concealed aboard—
BUT WHO IS DOING THIS THING?
I THINK A CRIME SYNDICATE IS AT WORK — AND I'M GOING TO LAY A LITTLE TRAP FOR THEM!
Later—
ANOTHER PEARL, MORGYN. EVEN FATTER THAN THE OTHER.
TONIGHT I SHALL KEEP IT IN MY TENT FOR SAFETY. TOMORROW I SHALL TAKE IT TO THE DEALER IN THE CITY.
That night—
OUR PLAN HAS WORKED. LOOKS LIKE SOME UNINVITED VISITORS HAVE ARRIVED.
URFF!
I ALWAYS KEEP A NICE WELCOME FOR UNINVITED GUESTS!
I DON'T LIKE PEOPLE WITH KNIVES!
AAAAAAAH!
UNLESS YOU WANT YOUR WRIST SNAPPED, YOU'D BETTER TELL ME WHO'S BEHIND THIS LITTLE EXPLOIT.
WE — WE DO NOT KNOW. WE HAVE TO MEET TWO PERSONS TOMORROW EVENING IN THE CASBAH AND HAND OVER THE PEARL. ONE WILL BE WEARING A FEZ, BOTH WILL BE IN WESTERN CLOTHES.

The following evening—
THERE ARE OUR CONTACTS, ALI. LET ME DO THE TALKING.
AS YOU WISH, MORGYN. YOU SPEAK MY LANGUAGE FLUENTLY.
Morgyn and Ali made the contact—
YOU HAVE WHAT WE HAVE COME TO COLLECT?
YOU HAVE THE MONEY? IF SO, HAND IT OVER FIRST.
The transaction was carried out—
GREEDY JACKALS!
NOW WE FOLLOW!
The men entered a nightclub. Morgyn and Ali slipped into the courtyard behind it—
IT'S SOME KIND OF OFFICE. I CAN SEE THROUGH A CHINK IN THE CURTAIN.
AH, YOU HAVE BROUGHT THE PEARL. IT IS A FAT BEAUTY.
WE PAID THE TWO MEN IN COUNTERFEIT MONEY, MEHMET ASSAT.
HE IS IN FOR A SURPRISE IN A MINUTE.
BAH! IDIOTS! CLOWNS! YOU HAVE BEEN FOOLED! IT IS A FAKE!
THAT'S RIGHT! A FAKE! AND I'VE GOT ALL THE EVIDENCE I NEED TO SEE YOU HANGED!

YOU THINK YOU'RE CLEVER, MORGYN. BUT YOU'VE MISJUDGED MEHMET ASSAT!
AND HOW WOULD THAT BE?
THAT'S HOW, MORGYN! I CANNOT TAKE TOO MANY PRECAUTIONS IN MY GAME.
WAAAAAAARGH!
STAY RIGHT WHERE YOU ARE!
Later, on board Assat's large dhow—
AS YOU ARE INTERESTED IN PEARL DIVING I DECIDED ON THE PERFECT END FOR YOU, MORGYN.
YOU HAVE A REAL HEART OF GOLD.
THE ONLY DIFFERENCE IS, THERE IS NO ONE TO PULL YOU BACK TO THE SURFACE!
WE'VE GOT ROUGHLY NINETY SECONDS TO GET OUT OF THIS!

SHARKS! I DOUBT IF THEY'LL WAIT THAT LENGTH OF TIME!
GOT TO HURRY! THOSE SHARKS ARE EDGING CLOSER!
MADE IT! NOW TO FREE ALI!
Morgyn freed Ali, seconds before one of the sharks decided to strike—
THIS STONE IS MY ONLY WEAPON!
THE OTHER SHARKS HAVE BEEN DRIVEN CRAZY BY THE SMELL OF THAT ONE'S BLOOD! THEY'RE TEARING IT TO PIECES!
On board the dhow—
THEY'RE TOO BUSY LOOKING FOR OUR MANGLED REMAINS TO SPOT US, ALI! LET'S SLIP BELOW DECK.

AAAAAAARGH!
THAT'S ONE LESS TO DEAL WITH LATER.
In the captain's cabin—
GUNS! THAT'S WHAT WE NEED!
But—
GRAB THEM!
BLAST! NO TIME TO LOAD!
THAT'S THE WAY, ALI! BUT THERE ISN'T ROOM FOR TWO OF US TO SWING A RIFLE!
SONS OF JACKALS! I'VE WAITED LONG TO DO THIS!
An oil lamp went flying—
AAAAAAH!
THE CABIN'S ON FIRE! I'M GETTING OUT OF HERE!
BUT MORGYN AND THE OTHERS WON'T!

THIS DESK IS OUR ONLY HOPE!
ALLAH BE WITH US, MORGYN. FIRE IS A TERRIBLE WAY TO DIE!
AS GOOD AS A TANK, THAT THING!
HE'S ESCAPING!
I DON'T THINK HE'LL GET FAR! FOLLOW ME!
HAPPY LANDINGS, ALI!
ALI'S MISJUDGED THINGS SLIGHTLY, BUT I'VE GOT HIM ALL RIGHT!
WELL DONE, MORGYN. THIS RAT WILL BE LOCKED AWAY FOR A LONG TIME!
AND THE PEARL THAT WAS STOLEN IS WAITING FOR YOU BACK AT ASSAT'S OFFICE. NOT A BAD DAY'S WORK!
THE END

PHOTO QUIZ

1. This is a scene from what Canadians often call the 'Greatest Outdoor Show on Earth'. What is the show?

2. How many players are there altogether in an American Football Team squad?

3. Do you know what this castle is?

4. No, it's not something from outer space! Do you know what it is?

5. How far did the Virgin Atlantic Challenger I get in its attempt to break the Atlantic speed record in 1985?

6. How do you fancy this dog for a pet? Do you know what it is?

7. Three very famous people — but what were their original names?

8. This horse won the Derby in 1983 and shortly afterwards was kidnapped. What was it called?

9. The only private army in Britain is on parade. Do you know who they are?

10. Feet and knees as well as fists are used in this form of boxing. What is it called?

ANSWERS

1. The Calgary Stampede. 2. 45. 3. Glamis Castle. 4. The Thames Barrier. 5. 138 miles from the finish. 6. A Pyrenean Mountain Dog. 7. Cliff Richard was born Harry Webb, Michael Caine was christened Maurice Micklewhite and Big Daddy was born Shirley Crabtree. 8. Shergar. 9. The Atholl Highlanders. 10. Thai boxing.

The JUNGLE WARRIOR
A TRUE STORY OF MEN AT WAR
BANZAI! BANZAI!
Colonel F. Spencer Chapman was a housemaster at Gordonstoun School, an explorer and a mountaineer. He became a soldier when he joined the local T.A. battalion o the Seaforth Highlanders early in 1939 and soon proved himself to be a natural-born warrior. By the end of 1941, during World War II, Spencer Chapman had helped to form a ski battalion, then joined the Special Training Centre in Scotland, before being posted to Australia to set up a guerrilla school there. He was running a similar special school in Malaya when the Japs attacked in December 1941.
As the Japs besieged Singapore, Spencer Chapman, now a Major, drove north in his scarlet Ford V8 coupe, with its dicky piled high with tommy guns and explosive packs. With him went Sergeant Sartin, an R.E. explosives instructor, and Bill Harvey, a rubber planter who had joined the Malay Volunteers. They were getting behind the enemy lines.
THERE'S A RUBBER ESTATE AND BUNGALOW A COUPLE OF MILES UP THE ROAD, MAJOR. WE CAN BED DOWN THERE IF THE NIPS HAVEN'T GOT THERE FIRST.
Soon they had ditched the car and gone into the jungle. They were already experts here, one man cutting the path, the next covering him, and the third keeping the course by compass.
KEEP A BIT MORE TO THE LEFT, SERGEANT. WE'RE GETTING OFF THE TRACK AGAIN.

Not even the jungle killers worried them.
JUST LET IT CARRY ON. IT'S WILD PIG HE'S AFTER, NOT WHITE MEN.
They established a hide-out base and early in January started their raids.
THAT'S THE BRIDGE, AND IT'S STRONGER THAN I EXPECTED. WE HAVEN'T ENOUGH EXPLOSIVE WITH US TO DEMOLISH IT, BUT THERE COULD BE ANOTHER WAY. COME ON!
MAJOR, I'VE BURIED THIRTY POUNDS OF PLASTIC EXPLOSIVE IN THE MIDDLE OF THE LINE.
RIGHT. NOW THE PRESSURE SWITCH BENEATH THE RAIL. WE ONLY WANT IT TO GO OFF WHEN THE TRAIN GOES OVER IT. WITH LUCK, IT'LL TAKE THE BRIDGE WITH IT.
Next, they walked back up the line setting smaller charges filled with time-pencil fuses at long intervals.
And soon afterwards —
GOT IT! NOW, HOLD YOUR BREATH — LET'S SEE IF OUR PLAN WORKS!
It worked!
AIEEEEE! AAAARGH!

As the Japs hurried to the wreck, the time-pencilled fuses began to work.
AAAH! IT IS MURDER!
To get back in daylight, they disguised themselves as Indian Tamil coolies, putting their uniforms and weapons into gunny sacks.
JAP OFFICERS! DON'T FORGET WHAT WE HAVE TO DO.
IGNORANT PEASANTS! BUT THEY KNOW WHO THEIR MASTERS ARE NOW.
Shortly afterwards, they were setting charges on another railway bridge, when —
LISTEN! THAT SOUNDED LIKE AN ENGINE WHISTLE. GATHER YOUR GEAR UP QUICK AND LET'S GET OFF THE BRIDGE. I DON'T WANT TO BE RUN OVER AS WELL AS BLOWN UP!
GOOD GRIEF, IT'S GOING TO BE A DARN CLOSE RUN THING!
Off the bridge, they jumped for their lives, but —
IT'S A SWAMP DOWN HERE!

The charge only damaged the engine which staggered on to the other end. Then —
RUN! RUN! IT WILL BLOW UP!
The Japs headed north at the double without seeing the guerrillas.
MIGHT AS WELL FINISH THE JOB BEFORE WE GO.
There were many Chinese guerrilla camps in the Malayan jungle and later Spencer Chapman lived with these enemies of the Japs, teaching them about weapons and unarmed combat.
THEN, BRING THE KNEE UP INTO THE MIDDLE OF THE BACK— HARD!
And when the battery torches ran out —
SEE? A FEW FIREFLIES PLACED INSIDE THE REFLECTOR BOWL GIVES YOU ENOUGH LIGHT TO READ A MAP.
AH, THAT VER' CLEVER!

Once he was captured by the Japs after stumbling into their camp when moving to a new location.
KILLY-KOLLACK! KILLY-KOLLACK!
ALL RIGHT, YOU'VE GOT ME. PUT YOUR GUNS DOWN.
They put him in a tent guarded by two sentries and an NCO. But at night, he burst out through the back of it.
AIEEEE!
With bullets chasing him, he crashed through a bamboo thicket —
He made good his escape, continuing to fight with the Chinese until the end of 1943, when British volunteers joined him, coming from Ceylon by submarine, and Liberator bombers flew thousands of miles to drop supplies to them.
In 1945, he travelled to Ceylon by submarine after 3½ years in the jungle, but returned in time to organise guerrilla help to Operation "Zipper", the proposed invasion of Malaya by the British. To get back, he made his first parachute drop.
IF I LAND ON TOP OF THE RUDDY TREES, I MAY AS WELL NEVER HAVE TRIED TO GET BACK!
But because Japan surrendered after the atom bombs had been dropped on them, Operation "Zipper" never took place. Spencer Chapman was promoted to full Colonel and awarded the DSO for his invaluable services behind the enemy lines.

GOLD FEVER!
In 1873, a wandering Ute Indian sighted three white men prospecting for gold in a canyon in Nevada . . .
DON'T WORRY, BOYS. HE WON'T BOTHER US WHEN HE SEES WE'VE GOT GUNS.
Duckwater Bill was breaking in two greenhorn partners . . .
THIS IS JUST A PLACER POCKET THAT'LL PAN OUT AT MAYBE TWO OR THREE THOUSAND DOLLARS. COULD BE A BIG LODE HIGHER UP, BUT THAT'LL TAKE SOME FINDING.
MEANWHILE WE ARE SHORT OF GRUB. ONE OF US HAS TO MAKE THE TRIP TO HOT SPRINGS.
LOOKS LIKE IT'S ME WHO'S DRAWN THE SHORT STRAW. I'D BETTER WAIT A COUPLE OF DAYS TILL WE'VE PANNED ENOUGH DUST TO PAY FOR THE GRUB.
BUD, SHOWING A GLEAM OF YELLOW IN ANY TOWN AROUND HERE WILL MEAN A MOB TAILING YOU WHEN YOU PULL OUT. WE HAVE TO SCRATCH UP EVERY LAST CENT WE HAVE AMONG US.

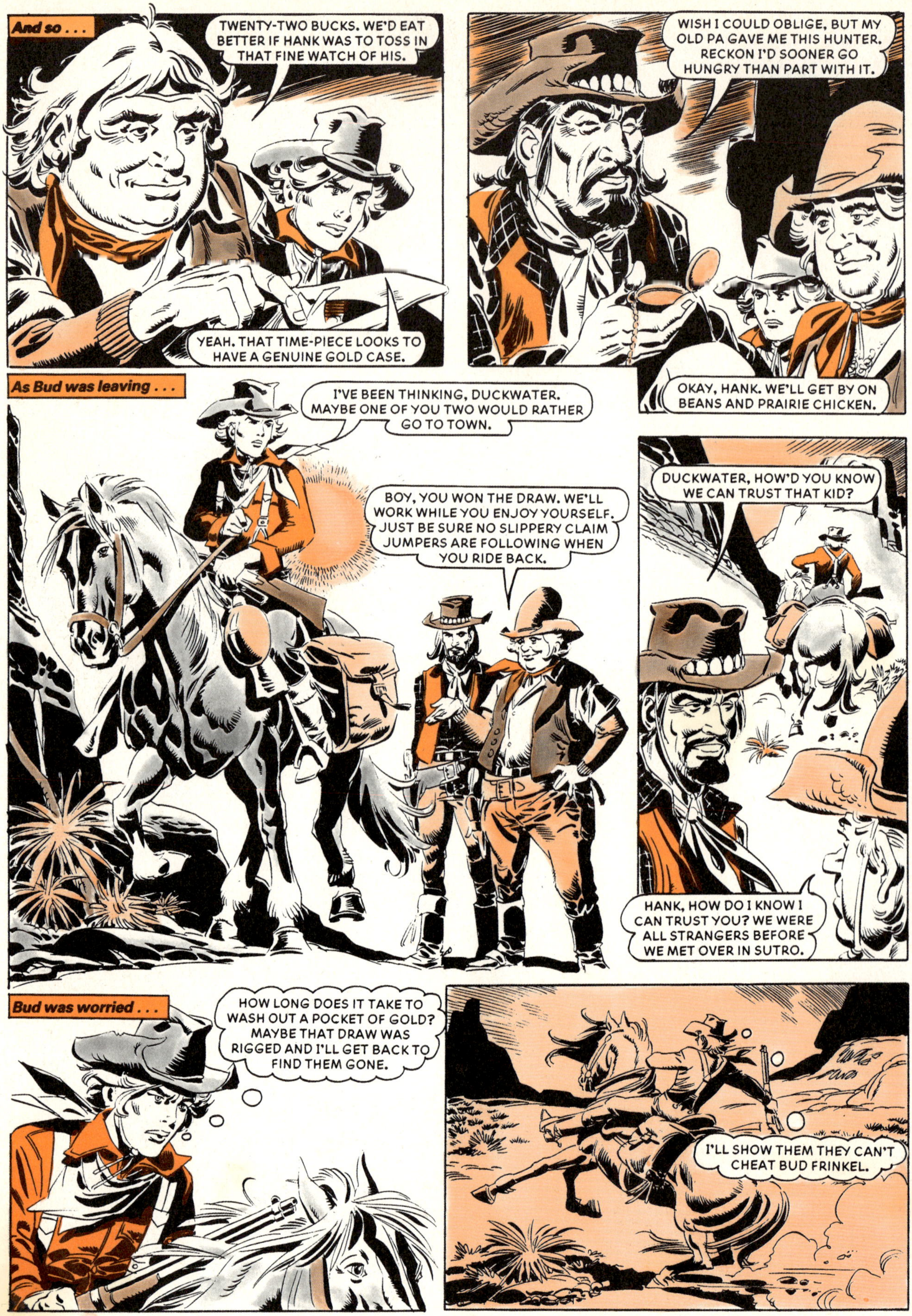

And so . . .
TWENTY-TWO BUCKS. WE'D EAT BETTER IF HANK WAS TO TOSS IN THAT FINE WATCH OF HIS.
YEAH. THAT TIME-PIECE LOOKS TO HAVE A GENUINE GOLD CASE.
WISH I COULD OBLIGE, BUT MY OLD PA GAVE ME THIS HUNTER. RECKON I'D SOONER GO HUNGRY THAN PART WITH IT.
OKAY, HANK. WE'LL GET BY ON BEANS AND PRAIRIE CHICKEN.
As Bud was leaving . . .
I'VE BEEN THINKING, DUCKWATER. MAYBE ONE OF YOU TWO WOULD RATHER GO TO TOWN.
BOY, YOU WON THE DRAW. WE'LL WORK WHILE YOU ENJOY YOURSELF. JUST BE SURE NO SLIPPERY CLAIM JUMPERS ARE FOLLOWING WHEN YOU RIDE BACK.
DUCKWATER, HOW'D YOU KNOW WE CAN TRUST THAT KID?
HANK, HOW DO I KNOW I CAN TRUST YOU? WE WERE ALL STRANGERS BEFORE WE MET OVER IN SUTRO.
Bud was worried . . .
HOW LONG DOES IT TAKE TO WASH OUT A POCKET OF GOLD? MAYBE THAT DRAW WAS RIGGED AND I'LL GET BACK TO FIND THEM GONE.
I'LL SHOW THEM THEY CAN'T CHEAT BUD FRINKEL.

Duckwater and Hank were busy . . .
THAT INDIAN'S GONE!
NOT BEING IN SIGHT DON'T MEAN THE VARMINT'S GONE, HANK. WE'D BETTER PUT THE HORSES ON A CLOSE TETHER TONIGHT.
Suddenly . . .
URGH!
WHAT THE . . ?
THAT DURNED INDIAN! HE MUST HAVE A RIFLE.
Then . . .
AARGH!
BY GLORY, I SURE SETTLED WITH THEM THIEVING RASCALS.
THERE'S HANK, BUT WHERE IS DUCKWATER? I KNOW I HIT HIM HARD.

HEY, DUCKWATER! IT WASN'T ME WHO DONE THAT SHOOTING. SHOW YOURSELF, OLD-TIMER.
SHUCKS, A BODY-SHOT OLD COOT IS NOTHING TO WORRY ABOUT. I'LL RUN OFF THE HORSES TO MAKE SURE HE GOES NO PLACE BEFORE HE CROAKS.
NOW I'LL TAKE THIS FINE WATCH WHICH YOU WERE TOO MEAN TO HAND OVER BEFORE, HANK.
I'LL FETCH IN THEM SUPPLIES BEFORE SETTLING TO WORKING MY FIND. NOTHING MUCH TO WASHING GOLD THE WAY OLD DUCKWATER SHOWED IT.
MURDERING LITTLE POLECAT . . . URHHH! SEEMS LIKE HE'S DONE FOR ME.
LORDY — THE UTE! NOW I'M GOING TO LOSE MY HAIR!

Later, in Hot Springs . . .
YESSIR, A GENUINE GOLD HUNTER AS WAS GIVE TO ME BY MY DEAR OLD PA.
THEN YOUR PA WAS NAMED J. T. LUKE ACCORDING TO THIS LETTERING. SAME NAME AS MY PARTNER WHO WAS ROBBED OF A WATCH JUST LIKE THIS WHEN HE WAS MURDERED LAST SPRING.
SON, THE MARSHAL WILL BE WANTING TO TALK TO YOU.
I GOT NOTHING TO SAY TO ANY LAWMAN.
THEN ALL I GOTTA SAY IS — THIS!
ARGHHHH!
Two months passed . . .
THERE LAYS THE KID, DUCKWATER. LOOKS LIKE YOU TEAMED UP WITH A PAIR OF KILLERS.
IT'LL TEACH ME TO BE CAREFUL NEXT TIME I CHOOSE PARTNERS.
BLACK HAND, I'D BE A DEAD MAN TOO IF YOU HADN'T TOTED ME TO THE BRADY TRADING POST. HALF MY GOLD FIND IS YOURS IF YOU WANT IT.
YELLOW IRON SICKNESS FOR WHITE MEN. YOU KEEP.
GOLD WOULD BE WASTED ON AN IGNORANT SAVAGE LIKE THAT, DUCKWATER.
I GUESS YOU'RE RIGHT, MARSHAL.
The End

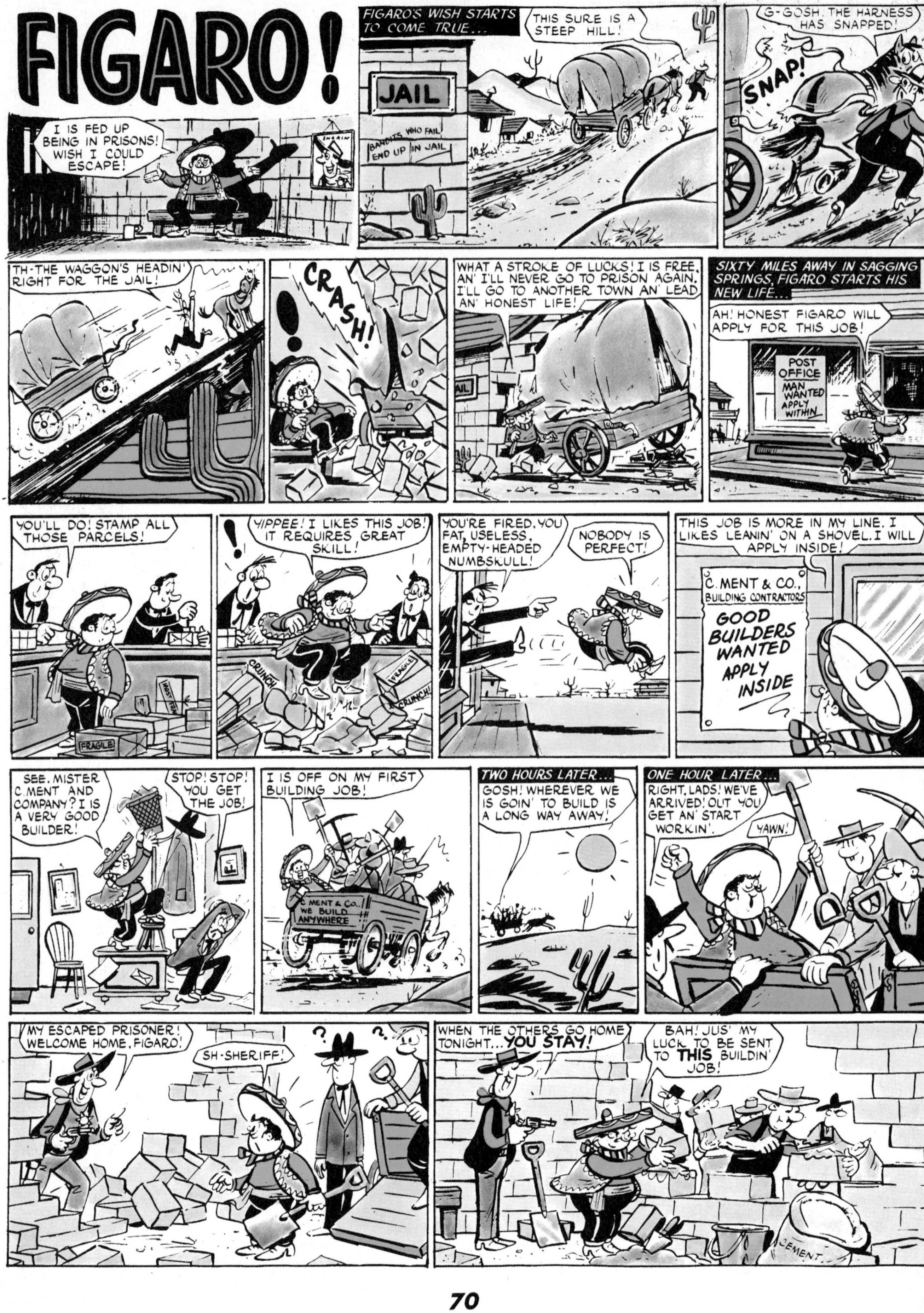
FIGARO!
I IS FED UP BEING IN PRISONS! WISH I COULD ESCAPE!
BANDITS WHO FAIL END UP IN JAIL
JAIL
FIGARO'S WISH STARTS TO COME TRUE...
THIS SURE IS A STEEP HILL!
G-GOSH. THE HARNESS HAS SNAPPED!
SNAP!
TH-THE WAGGON'S HEADIN' RIGHT FOR THE JAIL!
CRASH!
WHAT A STROKE OF LUCKS! I IS FREE. AN' I'LL NEVER GO TO PRISON AGAIN. I'LL GO TO ANOTHER TOWN AN' LEAD AN' HONEST LIFE!
SIXTY MILES AWAY IN SAGGING SPRINGS, FIGARO STARTS HIS NEW LIFE...
AH! HONEST FIGARO WILL APPLY FOR THIS JOB!
POST OFFICE
MAN WANTED APPLY WITHIN
YOU'LL DO! STAMP ALL THOSE PARCELS!
FRAGILE
YIPPEE! I LIKES THIS JOB! IT REQUIRES GREAT SKILL!
CRUNCH
FRAGILE
CRUNCH!
YOU'RE FIRED, YOU FAT, USELESS, EMPTY-HEADED NUMBSKULL!
NOBODY IS PERFECT!
THIS JOB IS MORE IN MY LINE. I LIKES LEANIN' ON A SHOVEL. I WILL APPLY INSIDE!
C. MENT & CO., BUILDING CONTRACTORS
GOOD BUILDERS WANTED APPLY INSIDE
SEE. MISTER C. MENT AND COMPANY? I IS A VERY GOOD BUILDER!
STOP! STOP! YOU GET THE JOB!
I IS OFF ON MY FIRST BUILDING JOB!
C. MENT & CO. WE BUILD ANYWHERE
TWO HOURS LATER...
GOSH! WHEREVER WE IS GOIN' TO BUILD IS A LONG WAY AWAY!
ONE HOUR LATER...
RIGHT, LADS! WE'VE ARRIVED! OUT YOU GET AN' START WORKIN'.
YAWN!
MY ESCAPED PRISONER! WELCOME HOME, FIGARO!
SH-SHERIFF!
?
?
WHEN THE OTHERS GO HOME TONIGHT... YOU STAY!
BAH! JUS' MY LUCK TO BE SENT TO THIS BUILDIN' JOB!
CEMENT

THE FLAG OF THE FEARLESS
In the Mediterranean Sea early in the Second World War, H.M. Submarine Fearless, captained by Lieutenant-Commander Rex Langley, was in action. She had just fired a salvo of torpedoes at three Italian cruisers . . .
Fearless did not wait to see the result of her attack. Even as the first torpedo struck home, she was diving deep . . .
Soon she settled on the sea bed, all her machinery switched off . . .
THERE GOES A DEPTH CHARGE NOW. BUT IT'S NOT TOO CLOSE.
THERE'S ANOTHER ONE — BUT IT'S FARTHER OFF.
THEN THEY'VE LOST US! LOOKS LIKE WE'VE MADE IT!

Leading Signalman Bill Mack decided to record the attack . . .
GETTING OUT THE JOLLY ROGER, EH, BILL?
MIGHT AS WELL SEW A TORPEDO ON IT. KEEP IT UP-TO-DATE.
H.M.S. FEARLESS
It was the custom for a British submarine to fly a Jolly Roger on returning to harbour after a war patrol. Bill Mack recorded the latest action by stitching a torpedo on the flag. A gun battle was denoted by a gun barrel. Long after Mack finished, Langley decided it was safe for Fearless to surface. It was now dark . . .
THERE'S AN OIL SLICK AND SOME WRECKAGE TO PORT. I THINK WE CAN CLAIM ONE CRUISER FOR SURE.
LOOK! MALTA'S COPPING IT AGAIN, SIR.
YES, IT'S TAKING A REAL PASTING THESE DAYS.
The Germans and Italians were doing all they could to destroy Malta and its important naval base. Fleets of bombers pounded the island day and night and enemy ships and submarines prowled the seas, eager to stop British convoys bringing supplies to the beleaguered garrison.
RADIO MESSAGE JUST RECEIVED, SIR.
WE'VE BEEN RECALLED FROM PATROL. WE'VE TO MAKE ALL SPEED BACK TO GIBRALTAR. PITY — WE'VE GOT TORPEDOES LEFT, TOO.
YES, WE MIGHT HAVE HELPED MALTA A BIT BY KEEPING THE ITALIANS AWAY FROM THE CONVOYS. STILL, ORDERS ARE ORDERS, I SUPPOSE.

A few days later, Fearless entered the anchorage at Gibraltar . . .
WELL, WE'LL SOON FIND OUT WHAT THIS IS ALL ABOUT.
Soon . . .
BLIMEY, WHAT'S ALL THIS LOT FOR?
DUNNO, BUT IF IT'S ALL FOR US IT SHOULD LAST A YEAR OR TWO!
As soon as Fearless left harbour again . . .
WE'RE ACTING AS ERRAND BOYS, DELIVERING A LOAD OF GROCERIES TO MALTA.
Two days from Malta . . .
PROPELLER NOISES, SIR! BEARING RED 30.
MOVING FAST AND CLOSING, SIR. SOUNDS LIKE A DESTROYER!
BLAST, SHE'S ON TO US!
The exploding depth charges caused chaos in Fearless . . .

WE'RE TAKING WATER AFT, SIR. IT'S AFFECTING THE BATTERIES OF THE ELECTRIC MOTOR AND CHLORINE GAS IS BUILDING UP!
ANY CHANCE OF CHECKING IT?
CAN'T GET NEAR THE LEAK, SIR. THERE'S TOO MUCH CHLORINE THERE ALREADY, AND MORE WATER'S COMING IN ALL THE TIME.
RIGHT THEN — WE'RE GOING UP! THE DESTROYER WILL BE WAITING FOR US. GUN CREW, CLOSE UP. BE READY FOR ACTION AS SOON AS WE BREAK SURFACE!
MAN THE GUN!
IT'S AN ITALIAN DESTROYER. LET'S GET IT BEFORE IT GETS US!
TAKE THAT, LUIGI!
A HIT!
But then . . .
AARGH!

GOOD, THE GUN'S STILL IN ACTION — BUT WE CAN'T TAKE MUCH MORE OF THIS!
BLIMEY, THIS IS HOT WORK!
THE GAS IS STILL SPREADING THROUGH THE BOAT! WE CAN'T LIVE DOWN THERE MUCH LONGER!
BRING EVERYONE UP, NUMBER ONE. STAND BY TO ABANDON SHIP!
THE DESTROYER'S ON FIRE FORWARD!
LOOK! THEY'RE ABANDONING SHIP TOO, SIR.
AYE, IT LOOKS LIKE WE'VE SUNK EACH OTHER!
Langley was the last man off Fearless . . .
SHE'S GOING DOWN!
THERE SHE GOES — ALONG WITH ALL THE STORES FOR MALTA!

LOOK AT THE ITIES! THEY'RE NOT GOING TO PICK US UP!
THEY'RE IN TOO MUCH OF A HURRY TO SAVE THEIR OWN SKINS.
LINK UP. FORM CIRCLES AND HELP TO SUPPORT ONE ANOTHER.
MIGHT AS WELL MAKE A PARTY OF IT. TAKE IT IN TURNS TO SING A SONG. THE BEST SINGER GETS A PRIZE.
OKAY, I'LL START, SIR. I KNOW SOME SMASHING SONGS ABOUT OFFICERS.
WAIT A MINUTE! LOOK AT THE DESTROYER, SIR. SHE LOOKS A LONG WAY FROM FINISHED TO ME!
MAYBE THE ITALIANS WERE IN TOO MUCH OF A HURRY TO LEAVE HER!
I THINK YOU'RE RIGHT. COME ON, LET'S FIND OUT!
THEY'VE LEFT PLENTY LINES FOR US TO CLIMB UP!
WE'VE MADE IT — BUT WHAT'S THAT ROUND YOUR MIDDLE, MACK?
OUR JOLLY ROGER, SIR. COULDN'T LEAVE IT BEHIND!

DAMAGE CONTROL PARTIES, NUMBER ONE. LET'S SEE WHAT WE CAN DO FOR THIS TUB.
The men split up into parties to explore the ship and see what damage had been done. Their report was encouraging. A section of the fore-part was flooded, but water-tight doors had prevented the flood from spreading. The engineers managed to raise pressure in the boilers and the pumps began to suck the water out of the flooded section. Soon it was apparent that the destroyer would be seaworthy enough for a short journey at least.
Langley called his crew together . . .
WE'RE SEAWORTHY ENOUGH FOR A SHORT JOURNEY AT LEAST. WE COULD HEAD DIRECT FOR MALTA, BUT WE'VE LOST THE CARGO OF FOOD WE WERE MEANT TO TAKE. MAYBE WE COULD GET MORE TO REPLACE IT!
GO RAIDING THE ITALIANS, YOU MEAN, SIR?
SICILY ISN'T FAR AWAY. WE COULD TRY A SMASH AND GRAB RAID THERE. BUT I'M GIVING YOU THE CHOICE, SINCE THERE'S PROBABLY NO FUTURE IN THIS LITTLE LARK.
I RECKON WE'D ALL LIKE TO STIR THE ITALIANS UP A BIT, SIR.
THAT WE WOULD!
So the destroyer, which was named "Il Duce", headed for Sicily . . .
SMALL BOATS OFF THE STARBOARD BOW, SIR!
IT'S THE CREW OF THIS DESTROYER, SIR! WHAT SHALL WE DO WITH THEM?
THEY'LL REACH LAND ALL RIGHT. LEAVE THEM WHERE THEY ARE.
KEEP ROWING, LUIGI. JUST A FEW MORE MILES!

Later, off the Sicilian port of Agrento . . .
THOSE HARBOUR GUNS WOULD BLOW US OUT OF THE WATER IF WE TRIED TO SNEAK IN. PITY WE DON'T KNOW THE IDENTIFICATION SIGNAL.
HEY, THERE'S A SHIP COMING OUT!
NO ESCORT WITH HER, SIR. THAT MEANS SHE'S ENGAGED IN COASTAL TRAFFIC, AND IS GOING TO SCUTTLE ALONG IN SIGHT OF LAND.
SHE'S LOW IN THE WATER, SO SHE'S CARRYING CARGO. WE'LL FIND OUT WHAT IT IS WHEN SHE'S WELL AWAY FROM THE PORT.
WE'LL HAVE TO GET RID OF THAT ITALIAN FLAG, THOUGH. AND THERE ISN'T A WHITE ENSIGN ABOARD.
International law required a ship to disclose her real identity when she went into action.
NO PROBLEM. MACK BROUGHT OUR JOLLY ROGER ALONG. WE'LL USE THAT!
And soon . . .
HEAVE TO OR I'LL PUT A SHELL INTO YOU! THIS IS A BRITISH SHIP!
MAMA MIA!

When they boarded the freighter . . .
A CATTLE BOAT!
THEY COULD USE SOME FRESH BEEF IN MALTA, SIR. SHALL WE TAKE HER IN TOW?
TOO SLOW. THE ALARM WILL BE GIVEN AS SOON AS THOSE SURVIVORS ARE PICKED UP, AND THEN WE'LL NEED ALL THE SPEED WE'VE GOT. NO, GET THOSE CATTLE ABOARD HERE.
EASY DOES IT NOW.
Later . . .
WE'VE RADIOED MALTA AND TOLD THEM WE'RE COMING. WE DON'T WANT OUR OWN PEOPLE TRYING TO SINK US!
AIRCRAFT COMING UP ASTERN, SIR. I DON'T THINK THEY'RE AFTER US, THOUGH. IT'S ANOTHER RAID ON MALTA.
ONE OF THEM'S SUSPICIOUS. DON'T FIRE UNLESS HE ATTACKS.
HE'S WHISTLED UP THREE OF THE BIG BOYS. AND SINCE WE CAN'T ANSWER THAT RECOGNITION SIGNAL WE'RE FOR IT NOW. ACTION STATIONS!

GOT 'IM!
SHIPS DEAD AHEAD, SIR.
THEY'RE OURS! MALTA'S SENT US AN ESCORT!
THEY'VE GOT BOTH OF THE BOMBERS, AND THE FIGHTER'S SHEERED OFF!
WE'RE AS GOOD AS HOME AND DRY!
The beleaguered Maltese cheered as "Il Duce" was escorted into the Grand Harbour at Valetta . . .
A PIRATE SHIP CARRYING CATTLE. THAT IS INDEED A STRANGE SIGHT — BUT A WELCOME ONE!
And Leading Signalman Mack had recorded the latest exploit of the Fearless's crew on the Jolly Roger!
HMS. FEARLESS
The End

NOT GOOD ENOUGH FOR CITY!
BURNHAM CITY FOOTBALL CLUB
MY NAME IS BILL POWELL AND I'M CHIEF SCOUT FOR FIRST DIVISION BURNHAM CITY. BUT THE FIRST TIME I MET DANNY DOBSON, I WAS STILL PLAYING FOR THE TEAM . . .
STANDS FGHJK
TICKET OFFICE
Danny was just five when the City adopted him as their mascot . . .
Danny's father, Fred, was our most devoted supporter and had great plans for the youngster . . .
THAT'S MY BOY!
As he grew up, Danny played regularly for his school team . . .
When Danny left school he played for a local amateur team and I had given up playing to take up my scouting job . . .
YOU KNOW IT'S ALWAYS BEEN MY AMBITION THAT DANNY WOULD PLAY FOR THE CITY, BILL. CAN YOU FIX HIM UP WITH A TRIAL?
NO PROBLEM, FRED. WE'LL GIVE HIM A RUN IN OUR YOUTH TEAM — THE COLTS!

I was up North on a scouting job and missed Danny's first few games for the Colts. But when I got back the manager, John Freeman, had a word with me . . .
IT'S ABOUT DANNY DOBSON, BILL. I'D LIKE YOU TO WATCH THE COLTS' NEXT MATCH WITH ME AND TELL ME WHAT YOU THINK.
OKAY, BILL. THEY PLAY AWAY TO UXPORT UNITED THIRD ELEVEN THIS SATURDAY MORNING.
So that Saturday . . .
I RECKON I KNOW WHAT JOHN'S WORRIED ABOUT!
YEP! THERE'S NO DOUBT ABOUT IT!
The game ended in a 0-0 draw . . .
WELL, BILL, WHAT DO YOU THINK?
I HATE TO SAY IT JOHN, BUT HE'S NOT GOOD ENOUGH. OH, HE'S A HARD WORKER AND NOT MUCH GETS PAST HIM, BUT HE LACKS THAT SPECIAL QUALITY WE'RE LOOKING FOR.
THAT'S JUST IT — HE'S AVERAGE! WELL I SUPPOSE WE'LL HAVE TO TELL HIM. IT'S NOT FAIR TO BUILD UP HIS HOPES.
I'LL TELL HIM, JOHN. I'M A FRIEND OF THE FAMILY AND HE MIGHT TAKE IT BETTER FROM ME.
And so . . .
DANNY, I'VE GOT SOME BAD NEWS, SON. CITY WON'T BE ASKING YOU TO SIGN ON. I'M AFRAID YOU'RE JUST NOT GOOD ENOUGH!
OH, NO!
HOW WILL I TELL DAD? HE'LL BE SHATTERED. HIS ONE AMBITION IN LIFE IS TO SEE ME PLAY FOR CITY.
YOUR DAD WILL BE AT OUR HOME GAME THIS AFTERNOON. I'LL COME WITH YOU WHEN WE GET BACK TO BURNHAM AND I'LL EXPLAIN IT TO HIM.

When we got back to Burnham, we headed straight for the ground . . .
THERE'S GOING TO BE SOME CROWD TODAY. GOOD JOB DAD ALWAYS GOES TO THE SAME SPOT ON THE TERRACING.
YEAH, OUR MEETING WITH WHITFIELD ROVERS COULD TURN OUT TO BE A LEAGUE DECIDER.
Outside the stadium . . .
LOOK, THERE'S DAD!
DANNY! BILL!
HOW'D THE GAME GO, DANNY? DID YOU WIN?
FRED! LOOK OUT! A CAR —
AAH!
DAD! OH, NO!
QUICK! GET AN AMBULANCE!
DAD! DAD!
Later, at the hospital . . .
Accident
Emergen
I'M AFRAID YOUR FATHER SUFFERED A SERIOUS FRACTURE OF THE SKULL AS WELL AS CUTS AND BRUISES.
CAN WE SEE HIM?

HE'S HOLDING HIS OWN AT THE MOMENT, BUT WHEN HE COMES ROUND HE'LL HAVE TO TAKE IT EASY FOR A WHILE. NO EXCITEMENT OF ANY KIND.
WE — WE CAN'T TELL HIM ABOUT MY NOT BEING TAKEN ON BY CITY, MR POWELL. HE COULDN'T TAKE IT!
THAT'S OKAY, DANNY. WE'LL WAIT UNTIL HE'S FULLY RECOVERED AND BREAK IT TO HIM GENTLY. IN THE MEANTIME WE'LL LET HIM THINK YOU'RE DOING WELL WITH THE CLUB.
But a few weeks later when I went round to visit Fred at his house . . .
I'M REALLY WORRIED, BILL. FRED'S NOT MAKING MUCH PROGRESS. THE DOCTOR'S VERY CONCERNED TOO.
I'LL HAVE A WORD WITH HIM, MARY, AND TRY TO CHEER HIM UP.
I'M GLAD YOU CAME, BILL. I WANTED TO ASK YOU HOW YOUNG DANNY'S GETTING ON WITH THE CITY.
HE'S DOING FINE, FRED. WHY DO YOU ASK?
I'M REALLY WORRIED ABOUT HIM, BILL. I DON'T RECKON HE'S GETTING ON AS WELL AS HE OUGHT TO. EVERY TIME I ASK HIM HE PUTS ME OFF.
LOOK, FRED, YOU CAN STOP WORRYING. IN FACT DANNY'S DONE SO WELL HE'S BEEN PICKED TO PLAY FOR THE FIRST TEAM AGAINST REDBURN TOMORROW.
BUT — HE NEVER MENTIONED IT TO ME!
ER — THAT'S BECAUSE HE DOESN'T KNOW YET. THE MANAGER JUST TOLD ME TODAY. SO YOU CAN STOP WORRYING AND GET BETTER QUICKLY! WE NEED OUR BEST SUPPORTER TO CHEER US ON!
A few minutes later . . .
IT WAS A SPUR OF THE MOMENT DECISION ON MY PART, DANNY, BUT YOU'LL HAVE TO BACK ME UP.
WE'LL NEVER GET AWAY WITH IT, MR POWELL. HE'S BOUND TO FIND OUT!
IT'LL WORK I TELL YOU. YOU CAN WATCH THE MATCH AND GIVE HIM A REPORT ON IT LATER. HE'S NOT ALLOWED TO READ THE PAPERS BECAUSE OF HIS HEAD INJURY AND THE RADIO COVERAGE IS VERY MINIMAL. WE'LL TELL HIM THE TRUTH WHEN HE'S STRONGER.
WELL, IF YOU'RE SURE, MR. POWELL . . .

I hurried round to City's ground . . .
AH, BILL. I'VE GOT A PROBLEM WITH THE TEAM SELECTION. GARY WALTERS HAS FAILED A FITNESS TEST . . .
Just then . . .
WE HAVE ALL OUR EQUIPMENT SET UP, MR FREEMAN. THANKS FOR YOUR CO-OPERATION.
WHAT EQUIPMENT? WHAT'S GOING ON?
OF COURSE YOU'VE BEEN OUT OF TOWN FOR THE LAST FEW DAYS AND DON'T KNOW ABOUT IT. WE'RE HAVING A SECOND-HALF RADIO COMMENTARY ON THE MATCH TOMORROW!
OH, NO! FRED'S BOUND TO BE LISTENING. HE'LL FIND OUT THAT DANNY'S NOT PLAYING!
ANYWAY WHAT ARE WE GOING TO DO ABOUT FILLING GARY'S PLACE IN THE MIDFIELD? HALF OUR RESERVE TEAM ARE DOWN WITH FLU.
PLAY DANNY DOBSON!
I explained about Fred . . .
BUT — BUT DANNY'S NOT GOOD ENOUGH! YOU AGREED!
I KNOW HE'S NOTHING SPECIAL, BUT HE WON'T LET US DOWN. AND IT WILL REALLY HELP TO GET FRED ON HIS FEET AGAIN.
I DON'T KNOW, BILL. IT'S TAKING AN AWFUL CHANCE.
LOOK, JOHN. WE'RE LYING SECOND IN THE LEAGUE AND REDBURN ARE DOWN AT THE BOTTOM. WE SHOULD BEAT THEM EASILY ENOUGH EVEN WITH DANNY IN THE TEAM.
WELL, OKAY, BILL, BUT IF WE LOSE I'LL HAVE YOUR HIDE!
WE WON'T, JOHN, I PROMISE YOU. I'LL GO AND TELL DANNY.

I rushed back to Danny's house . . .
I — I CAN'T, MR POWELL. I'M NOT GOOD ENOUGH! I'LL LET THE TEAM DOWN.
NO YOU WON'T, DANNY. AND YOU'VE GOT TO DO IT FOR YOUR DAD'S SAKE!
WELL, IF YOU PUT IT LIKE THAT — I DON'T HAVE MUCH CHOICE!
GOOD LAD. SEE YOU TOMORROW!
Next afternoon . . .
ISN'T THAT FRED DOBSON'S SON AT NUMBER SIX?
YEAH. A BIT OF A SURPRISE THAT. I DIDN'T KNOW YOUNG DANNY WAS EVEN PLAYING FOR THE RESERVES. STILL, I BET FRED'S PROUD AS PUNCH.
As the game started —
I HOPE I'VE DONE THE RIGHT THING. IT MIGHT BE TOO MUCH FOR DANNY.
Redburn swept into the attack . . .
GREAT PASS, TOMMY!
But . . .
WELL CUT OUT, SON.
And shortly . . .
MY BALL!

YOUR BALL, GEORGE.
GOOD PASS, DANNY.
From the winger's cross . . .
YES! UP THE CITY!
YOUNG DANNY DOBSON MADE THAT!
And during the second-half . . .
AND YOUNG DANNY DOBSON HAS GROWN IN MATURITY AND CONFIDENCE AS THE GAME HAS PROGRESSED. HE COULD BE A REAL FIND FOR CITY.
HE'S BEGINNING TO LOOK A BIT SPECIAL AFTER ALL, BILL.
CAR HIR
YOU CAN SAY THAT AGAIN. MUST BE BECAUSE HE'S PLAYING TO HELP HIS DAD GET WELL. NOW, DANNY — PASS!
HIT IT, MIKE!
IT'S THERE! THANKS TO ANOTHER DEFENCE-SPLITTING PASS FROM DOBSON!

With only minutes to go . . .
BACK TO ME!
SHOOT, DANNY! SHOOT!
And at Danny's house . . .
YES! WHAT A GOAL!
AND DANNY DOBSON ROUNDS OFF A SUPERB PERFORMANCE WITH ONE OF THE FINEST GOALS I'VE SEEN THIS SEASON!
YOU SHOW 'EM, DANNY!
TO THINK WE NEARLY LET HIM GO, BILL.
AYE, JOHN, BUT I RECKON YOUNG DANNY DOBSON WILL BE WITH CITY FOR A LONG TIME TO COME NOW.
Fred made a speedy recovery after that and was soon back on the terracing watching his dream come true . . .
UP THE CITY! COME ON, DANNY!
DANNY DOBSON IS NOW SKIPPER OF BURNHAM CITY. WHICH JUST GOES TO SHOW THAT EVEN PROFESSIONAL SCOUTS CAN MAKE MISTAKES!
The End

CADMAN
THE FRONT-LINE COWARD

STAND-TO ON THE FIRE-STEPS! GET THAT LEWIS GUN INTO ACTION!
TAKE COVER IN THIS DUG-OUT!
Soon a savage trench battle developed—
VORWARTS! ATTACK!
HOLD 'EM OFF, LADS!
SHOULDN'T YOU BE OUT THERE WITH YOUR MEN, CAPTAIN?
NOTHING I'D LIKE BETTER! BUT I AM UNDER STRICT ORDERS TO PROTECT YOU PRESS PEOPLE.
HUNS WITHDRAWING. SAFE TO COME OUT NOW.

DID YOU MAKE THIS STUPID RAID TO FIND OUT OUR STRENGTH HERE?
WE ALSO FOUND OUT THE TOMMIES HAVE A COWARD IN COMMAND!
INSOLENT HUN! GOOD MIND TO SHOOT YOU!
NOT WITH THOSE NEWSPAPER BLOKES HERE, SIR!
YOU SEEM TO SPEAK VERY GOOD GERMAN, CAPTAIN.
USEFUL FOR INTERROGATING PRISONERS.
A GERMAN-SPEAKING COWARD IN COMMAND ON THIS SECTOR MAY ALSO COME IN USEFUL FOR OTHER PURPOSES!
At Christmas, a few days later—
WHAT THE DEUCE ARE THOSE FELLOWS DOING, SMITH?
JERRIES SANG US SOME CAROLS SO WE'RE SINGING 'EM ONE BACK.
HUN OFFICER WAVING A WHITE FLAG!
OUR GALLANT CAPTAIN'S USUALLY BETTER AT THAT THAN THE ENEMY!
CHRISTMAS GREETINGS, HERR KAPTAIN! I AM MAJOR VON STAHL. MAY WE INVITE YOU AND YOUR MEN TO A DAY OF PEACE AND GOODWILL?
JUST AS HAPPENED EARLIER ON IN THE WAR!
SO IT DID, BY GAD!

So soon—
CIGARETTES, TOMMY?
CHOCOLATES, FRITZ?
YOU AND YOUR CORPORAL MUST JOIN ME AND MY SERGEANT FOR SOME FOOD AND DRINKS AT OUR COMPANY HQ.
WITH PLEASURE, HERR MAJOR!
BIT ODD, SIR! THAT JERRY SERGEANT TALKS GOOD ENGLISH. HE WAS BOASTING TO ME ABOUT ALL THE MEDALS HIS MAJOR HAS WON IN SOME RATHER NASTY ACTIONS.
SO WHAT? I HAVE MEDALS, TOO!
YES, BUT THIS JERRY OFFICER REALLY WON HIS AWARDS! HE'S FROM A TOUGH PRUSSIAN GUARD UNIT WHO DON'T OFTEN MIX LIKE THIS WITH THE ENEMY . . .
In the German dug-out—
TRY OUR GERMAN CIGARS AND BRANDY.
HAVE SOME SCOTCH WHISKY!
CHEERS WITH A MUG OF BEER, SARGE!
EXCUSE US A MOMENT! MY SERGEANT AND I MUST CHECK THAT OUR MEN ARE BEHAVING THEMSELVES PROPERLY.
While the Germans were gone—
THOSE PAPERS! MARKED 'SECRET'! NO HARM IN TAKING A PEEP, EH?
GEHEIM
UNLESS THEY CATCH YOU AT IT! I'LL KEEP A LOOKOUT!

GAD! THESE ARE DETAILED PLANS FOR A HUN SURPRISE ATTACK ON THE ROSSEL SECTOR TOMORROW NIGHT!
GEHEIM
THAT PART OF THE FRONT'S HELD BY ONE OF OUR OTHER COMPANIES.
Later—
BACK TO OUR OWN LINES NOW. BUT LET US MAKE THIS TRUCE LAST A WHILE.
WE WON'T SHOOT IF YOU DON'T!
I'VE SEEN THAT BLOKE BEFORE . . .
I SPOTTED A JERRY OFFICER, SPITTING IMAGE OF ONE OF THOSE NEWSPAPER BLOKES, SIR. SCAR ON HIS FACE AND—
MANY HUN OFFICERS HAVE SUCH SCARS FROM FIGHTING MOCK SWORD DUELS AT THEIR COLLEGES.
BUT SUPPOSE IT WAS THE SAME BLOKE? SUPPOSE HE'S A SPY? WHAT IF HE SNEAKED OVER TO FIND OUT IF YOU'D JUMP AT A FAKE TRUCE?
SUCH DRIVEL! HOW COULD ANYONE KNOW I'D AGREE TO A TRUCE?
'COS HE SHOWED HIMSELF IN HIS USUAL BLUE FUNK, THAT'S WHY!
MAKE WAY! I MUST REPORT TO THE COLONEL!
At battalion HQ—
CLEVER WORK, CAPTAIN! AGREEING TO A TRUCE TO SPY ON ENEMY PLANS. WE'LL NOW MOVE THREE COMPANIES INTO THE THREATENED ROSSEL SECTOR, LEAVING JUST TWO PLATOONS IN YOUR OWN BOUVAY TRENCHES.
At dusk next day—
STILL ALL NICE AND QUIET, SMITH.
SO HOW ABOUT US OCCUPYING THAT OLD FORWARD OBSERVATION POST OUT THERE, SIR?
IT'S STILL LINKED BY TELEPHONE WIRE TO THE COMMAND POST. FROM THERE YOU COULD HELP DIRECT GUNFIRE WHEN THE JERRIES ATTACK ON THE OTHER SECTORS. BE ANOTHER FEATHER IN YOUR CAP, EH?
YES — ER — NOT A BAD IDEA. BUT YOU GO FIRST TO CHECK THAT THE HUNS ARE STILL KEEPING TO THE TRUCE.

JERRY'S STILL ALL CHUMMY, SEE? PROBABLY RECKON WE'RE OUT TO PICK UP STUFF LEFT BEHIND OUT HERE DURING YESTERDAY'S TRUCE PARTY.
GET THAT FIELD PHONE WORKING SIR, WHILE I NIP OUT TO SEE WHAT'S GOING ON IN OUR JERRY CHUMS' TRENCHES.
DON'T GIVE ME ORDERS, SMITH! AND DON'T GO ANNOYING THOSE HUNS!
JERRIES MADE THESE GAPS IN THEIR WIRE FOR OUR BLOKES TO GET THROUGH YESTERDAY. THEY'RE ALSO BLINKING HANDY FOR THE JERRIES THEMSELVES TO NIP OUT SMARTLY FOR A SURPRISE ATTACK.
HALT! GO BACK OR WE SHOOT, TOMMY!
NOW THAT'S NOT VERY FRIENDLY, CHUMS!
ACHTUNG! GRENADE!
JUST A SMOKE BOMB, FRITZ.
STREWTH! JAM-PACKED WITH JERRIES ALL SET TO GO OVER THE TOP! PRUSSIAN GUARDS FROM THE LOOK OF 'EM, TOO!
OPEN FIRE! THAT ENEMY SCOUT MUST NOT ESCAPE!
OUR SCAR-FACED CHUM AGAIN! I DON'T NEED MUCH GERMAN TO GUESS WHAT HE'S ON ABOUT!
GAD! I TOLD YOU NOT TO ANNOY THEM!
THEY'RE VERY TOUCHY, SIR! A WHOLE BATTALION OF THEIR BEST TROOPS PACKED INTO A COMPANY TRENCH!

VORWARTS! ATTACK THE POST!
NOW WE'RE BACK TO THE REAL BOMB-SLINGING GAME!
WHO GAVE YOU ORDERS TO FIRE WARNING FLARES?
YOU DID — IF YOU HAD ANY SENSE!
Moments later—
THAT SIGNAL FLARE'S SET OFF OUR OWN ARTILLERY DEFENCE BARRAGE!
JUST IN TIME!
AAAGH! GET BACK TO COVER.
IN YOU COME, CHUM! YOU'RE JUST THE BLOKE I WANT OUR CAPTAIN TO MEET!
RECOGNISE HIM NOW, SIR?
GAD! THAT NEWSPAPER REPORTER!
I AM HAUPTMANN BAUER OF OUR ARMY INTELLIGENCE. YOU CANNOT PROVE I SPIED AS A CIVILIAN ANY MORE THAN I CAN PROVE YOU ARE A COWARD.
WELL — ER — YOU CAN BE JUST A CAPTURED PRISONER AS FAR AS I'M CONCERNED.
I'VE SIGNALLED HQ TO MOVE THE BARRAGE FORWARD ON TO THE ENEMY FRONT LINES — AS YOU ORDERED, SIR.
ABOUT TIME! BEFORE WE GET BLOWN TO BITS BY OUR OWN GUNS!

THAT'LL KEEP JERRY'S HEAD DOWN WHILE WE NIP BACK TO OUR OWN LINES.
Soon—
THE COLONEL ACTED ON YOUR ORDERS, CAPTAIN, AND SENT STRONG REINFORCEMENTS BACK TO THIS SECTOR. THAT CAPTURED ENEMY OFFICER HAS ADMITTED THAT YOUR TRENCHES WERE THE REAL TARGET OF THEIR ATTACK.
TYPICAL HUN TRICK! I SUSPECTED IT ALL ALONG, MAJOR!
HERE THEY COME, LADS! BUT I DON'T RECKON THEY'LL PUSH IT FAR NOW.
THEY WON'T TRY THAT AGAIN IN A HURRY.
NOT NOW THEY KNOW WHAT THEY'RE UP AGAINST HERE, BY GAD!
OUR COLONEL WILL WISH TO COMMEND YOU FOR THE RISKS YOU TOOK IN ALL THIS, CAPTAIN.
WONDER IF THEY'VE GOT ANY CADMANS IN THE JERRY ARMY? IF SO, THEY MUST HAVE SHOT 'EM ALL, OR WE'D HAVE WON THIS BLINKING WAR YEARS AGO!
The End

THE HAMMER MAN

METHINKS THE KING IS NOT YET IN A FESTIVE MOOD. I HAVE A NOTION WHEREBY WE MAY GAIN HIS FAVOUR!
I HAVE HEARD THE KING SPEAK OF HIS WISH TO HAVE A YULETIDE TREE AS IS THE CUSTOM IN SOME FOREIGN LANDS. HENCE LET US MOVE THIS FINE FIR TO THE CASTLE COURTYARD.
HUP!
WHERE GO WE? I CANNOT SEE FOR THE TREE.
I'LL GUIDE YOUR WAY.
THE HOLLY AND THE IVY . . .
HAVE A CARE FOR THESE CAROL-SINGING NOBLES. NOW SWING IT AROUND.
KERRASH!
OOOPS! YOU SWUNG IT THE WRONG WAY!
SEE THE FINE FIR WE HAVE BROUGHT YOU, SIRE!
GADS GRIPES! I SEE NAUGHT BUT DIRE DAMAGE!
THAT FIR I PLANTED IN MY CHILDHOOD TO MARK THE GRAVE OF A MUCH-LOVED PET DOG. NOT ONLY HAVE YOU DESECRATED HIS TOMB BUT ALSO WRECKED THE WINDOW OF OUR BANQUET ROOM.

HOWEVER, NOW 'TIS HERE, PLANT IT IN THE COURTYARD, AND, WHILE YOU ARE ABOUT IT — PLANT YOURSELVES AS WELL!
ODDS BONES! 'TIS HARD LABOUR TO DIG IN THESE COURTYARD STONES!
YET SUCH A TREE NEEDS A GOODLY HOLE.
SWOOOSH!
OH, WOE! A WATER FLOW!
PERCHANCE YOU SMOTE A CHANNEL FROM A WELL! RAM THE TREE IN HEFTILY TO STEM THE LEAK!
NOW TO THE FROZEN RIVER THAMES FOR THE MERRY SPORT OF SKATING!
OOW!
AAAH!
GADZOOKS! THEY SKATE ALREADY!
HOW CAME THIS SHEET OF ICE HERE TO MAKE US SLIP?
BEST TELL HIM NOT 'TWAS OUR FROZEN WATER DRIP!
Soon, down by the frozen river . . .
'TWILL OFFEND THE KING MORE IF WE DO NOT JOIN IN ALL THE JOLLITIES, BUT WE HAVE NO SKATES.
I WILL FORGE SOME IN THE CASTLE SMITHY!

I WILL RE-SHAPE OLD SWORD AND DAGGER BLADES.
THEN STRAP THEM ON WITH HARNESS LEATHERS.
So, before long . . .
ODDS WOBBLES! I AM NOT WELL VERSED IN THIS SKATING SPORT.
THERE IS NAUGHT TO IT! FOLLOW ME!
STEAM FROM THE ICE! IN OUR HASTE WE DONNED THE BLADES WHILE STILL HOT FROM THE FORGE!
I FORGED THE BLADES TOO SHARPLY! THEY CUT LIKE SWORDS!
AAH! I FALL!
BLAMM!
KERRACK!
REMOVE THE SKATES BEFORE WE DO A MISCHIEF!
YEEAAAGH!
TOO LATE! WE HAVE CUT THE ICE FROM UNDER THE KING!

HERE, SIRE! TAKE MY HAMMER! GADS TEETH! I SKID!
CLONK!
OOOF!
SAINTS PRESERVE ME FROM THAT TWAIN! LET THEM NE'ER DARKEN OUR CHRISTMAS FESTIVITIES AGAIN!
That evening . . .
ODDS GRIPES! BANNED FROM THE BANQUET!
WE LACK EVEN SHELTER FROM THE SNOWY NIGHT!
But near a shed outside the castle walls . . .
PRAY SHELTER IN MY HUMBLE ABODE.
A KINDLY OFFER WE'LL NOT REFUSE.
I AM SILAS PAYNE, A POOR ALCHEMIST. THIS FOWL IS ALL I CAN AFFORD FOR YULETIDE FARE.
ODDS POVERTY! 'TIS NOBLE OF YOU TO SHARE IT WITH US!

I HOPE TO MAKE MY FORTUNE WITH THIS LATEST INVENTION. 'TIS CALLED A CRACKLER. MUCH MERRIMENT IS GAINED BY PULLING IT APART BETWEEN TWO PERSONS AT A BANQUET.
GIVE HOLD HERE, THEN!
MERELY A PINCH OF GUNPOWDER FUSE AND A TWIST OF PAPER.
BANG!
AAH!
THEN FROM THE CRACKLERS COME PAPER HATS AND CROWNS FOR MUCH MERRIMENT.
A MERRY DEVICE, FORSOOTH, AND SURELY THE ONLY CROWN LIKELY E'ER TO ADORN MY PATE!
A CRACK FOR YOUR CROWN, KING HAMMER-HEAD!
WHAM!
OOOF!
Minutes later . . .
ODDS STARS! WHAT HAPPENED?
WE WERE ASSAILED BY TWO NOBLES AND LEFT TRUSSED UP LIKE THIS!
OFF WITH THESE FETTERS!
'TWILL BE OFF WITH THE KING'S HEAD IF HE PULLS A CRACKLER LIKE THAT ONE YONDER!
I FASHIONED SUCH A PAIR AS A GIFT FOR THE KING. THOSE NOBLES WHO ASSAILED US TOOK ONE AND STUFFED IT FULL OF GUNPOWDER LIKE A BOMBSHELL! THEY PLAN TO GET THE KING TO BLOW HIMSELF UP!
WE MUST HASTE TO SAVE GOOD KING HAL.
BUT HOW SHALL WE KNOW WHICH NOBLES DID THIS DIRE DEED?
THEY WENT OFF WEARING MY CRACKLER PAPER CROWNS TO APPEAR AS MERRY-MAKERS AT THE ROYAL BANQUET.

THE BANQUET HALL DOOR IS BARRED TO US!
NOT FOR LONG! OLD IRONHEAD WILL SOON OPEN IT!
BEGONE! YOU ARE BANNED!
KNOCK ANY NOGGINS WEARING PAPER CROWNS!
LOOK! PAPER CROWNED HEADS!
NOT JUST TWO BUT THREE OF THE KNAVES!
YAAOW! TREASON!
OOF!
EURH!
ODDS CROWNS! THE THIRD IS GOOD KING HAL'S!
ENOUGH'S ENOUGH! CAST THESE KNAVES INTO OUR DEEPEST DUNGEON!
NAY, SIRE! WE COME TO SAVE YOU FROM PULLING THIS CRACKLER BOMBSHELL!
STOP! YOU ARE UNDER ARREST!
OUT OF OUR WAY, NOBLE OAFS!

In the courtyard . . .
OOPS! I SLIP ON THE ICE!
GADS BLASTS! THE CRACKLER IS PULLED!
Next moment . . .
YEEARGH!
BOOOM!
FORSOOTH, 'TWOULD SEEM YOU TWAIN DID TRULY SAVE ME FROM A FEARSOME BLAST! BUT WHERE IS BARON CHELL?
BLOWN TO BITS, ALAS!
NAY, HE IS UP THERE, ADORNING OUR YULETIDE TREE AS IN SOME FOREIGN LANDS SUCH TREES ARE ADORNED BY FAIRY DOLLS — A DAINTY CUSTOM WE MAY SOON COPY!
Later . . .
THE REBELLIOUS BARONS WHO PLOTTED MY DOOM HAVE CONFESSED THEIR TREASON PLOT. IT BEING CHRISTMAS I MAY EVEN FORGIVE THEIR FOUL FELONY AS I PARDON YOU TWAIN'S FORMER MISDEEDS.
GULP! SLURP!
NOW LET US SING A MERRY CAROL TO OUR KING! HEY, TRA-LA-LA-LAH!
ODDS EARDRUMS! MAYHAP I SHOULD THROW HIM IN THE DUNGEONS AFTER ALL!
THE END

SPORTING SMILES
I KNOW THIS IS SUPPOSED TO BE THE BIG MATCH, BUT THIS IS RIDICULOUS!
WAIT TILL YOU SEE THE SIZE OF THE GOALIE!
SURE IT'S ME IRISH JIG THAT SENDS 'EM REELING!
I ONLY WEAR THIS TO FRIGHTEN THE OPPOSITION!
HOW DO YOU GET YOUR CHIN SO SMOOTH, PAT?
THE WAY YOU LOT PLAY IN FRONT OF ME, LIAM, I ALWAYS HAVE PLENTY OF CLOSE SHAVES!
AND FURTHERMORE . . .
OUCH! DON'T YOU EVER CUT YOUR NAILS?
DON'T MIND US, SON. WE'RE JUST "CUEING" TO GET ON NEXT!
OTHERWISE WE'D HAVE TO TAKE POT-LUCK!
YOU WON'T CATCH ME MAKING ROTTEN JOKES LIKE THAT!
OR MEO!!

A CASE OF COINCIDENCE

IT'S ALL RIGHT NOW, LAD! A FEW BRUISES WON'T EVEN KEEP YOU FROM SCHOOL.
WE DID IT, WITH BUT SECONDS TO SPARE!
THE GALLANT ENGLISHMAN SHOULD GET A MEDAL FOR WHAT HE DID THIS DAY.
HE GETS THE ETERNAL THANKS FROM ME, UNCLE OF YOUNG ANTON. WHAT YOU DID TODAY I SHALL EVER RECALL WITH FERVENT GRATITUDE.
Two days later —
CHAP TO SEE YOU, SIR. LITTLE FRENCH BLOKE. SAYS HE WON'T GO AWAY UNTIL HE HAS SEEN THE SO GALLANT OFFICER LEE.
EH? NOW WHAT COULD A FRENCH CHAP WANT WITH ME? DON'T OWE ANY BILLS IN TOWN.
I CANNOT LET YOUR BRAVERY GO UNREWARDED, AND AS THE TOWN SILVERSMITH I CAN EXPRESS MY GRATITUDE SO.
OH, CRIKEY! OFFEND THE OLD BOY NO END IF I DON'T TAKE IT. BUT I DIDN'T WANT ALL THIS FUSS!
To a gallant ally from a grateful Frenchman
M.A. DULUC - RENECOURT
1918
I AM HONOURED TO ACCEPT YOUR GIFT AND I SHALL CARRY IT WHEREVER I GO.
MAY IT BRING YOU LUCK, MY FRIEND AND HELP YOU TO SURVIVE THIS SO TERRIBLE WAR.

A few days later—
THAT LITTLE FRENCHMAN SAID THE CASE WOULD BRING ME LUCK. IN THIS GAME I NEED ALL I CAN GET!
A week later—
THIS STRAFING LARK IS A BIT HAIRY. THEY CHUCK EVERYTHING UP AT YOU.
SCHWINE! HELMUT KUTZ DOES NOT RUN LIKE THE RABBIT FROM THE HAWK.
ARGHHHH! I'M HIT. THAT FELT LIKE A BLOW FROM A SLEDGE HAMMER. BETTER GET BACK!
YOU LOOK A BIT SHOOK UP, SIR. WAS IT A BAD RAID?
IT COULD HAVE BEEN MY LAST, OLD BOY. THAT IS AS CLOSE TO GETTING THE CHOP AS I WANT TO GET!
THIS CASE TOOK THE FORCE OF THAT BULLET!
I HEARD THAT FRENCH CHAP SAY THIS WOULD BRING YOU LUCK, AND IT MOST SURELY DID TODAY.
A few days later—
HEARD THE NEWS, JIM, OLD SON? IT'S OVER. WE CAN ALL GO HOME. OLD FRITZ HAS JACKED IT IN.
THANK GOODNESS FOR THAT. LET'S HOPE THAT WE CAN HAVE PEACE FOR GOOD NOW!

But the years passed, and brought yet another war.
BEFORE YOU LEAVE FOR YOUR FIRST OPERATIONAL SQUADRON, I WANT YOU TO HAVE THIS, FRANK. AND I HOPE IT BRINGS YOU THE LUCK IT DID ME.
THANKS, DAD. AND IF I DO HALF AS GOOD AS YOU DID I SHALL HAVE NOTHING TO BE ASHAMED OF.
SEPTEMBER, 1940. AND HUN HUNTING IS NOW IN SEASON. THAT BLIGHTER WON'T BE LAYING EGGS.
DONNERWETTER! AND THEY TOLD US THE R.A.F. HAD NO GOOD FIGHTERS.
Later . . .
THE BATTLE OF BRITAIN OVER, AND I BAGGED NINE WITHOUT A SCRATCH! THIS CASE REALLY SEEMS TO BRING LUCK AT THAT.
OVERSEAS HERE WE COME. LET'S HAVE ANOTHER BASH AT OLD JERRY IN SOME FOREIGN CLIME, OLD CHAPS.
In North Africa—
ACH! TWO LIKELY CANDIDATES FOR THE CHOP. THEY WILL NEVER KNOW WHAT HIT THEM.
WHAT A BORE! SIX WEEKS IN THE DESERT AND WE HAVEN'T SEEN THE OLD LUFTWAFFE ONCE.
LOOK OUT, LEE. BANDITS AT — ARGHHHH!
ONE DOWN AND KURT AND CARL SHOULD HAVE DOWNED THE OTHER BY NOW.
THAT'S FOR HARRY, BUT THOSE OTHER TWO ARE AFTER MY HIDE.

HECK! I'LL HAVE TO HIT THE SILK BEFORE I FRY. THAT BLIGHTER WAS REALLY HOT STUFF TO GET ON MY TAIL LIKE THAT!
ACH! HE GOT MEIN KAMERADEN BUT HE WILL NOT REACH HIS BASE TO BOAST ABOUT IT.
DIDN'T GET A RADIO CALL OFF BEFORE THOSE JOHNNIES BOUNCED ME!
Two hours later—
CAN'T KEEP ON MUCH LONGER. THIS HEAT SUCKS ALL THE LIFE OUT OF A MAN. SEEMS THE CASE JUST LOST ITS POWERS AS FAR AS I'M CONCERNED.
THAT'S IT. I'VE HAD IT. JUST A MATTER OF TIME NOW. SO MUCH FOR DAD'S LUCKY CASE. DIDN'T DO ME A LOT OF GOOD IN THE END.
Later—
STEADY ON. WHEN I PUT THIS TO YOUR LIPS, DRINK VERY SPARINGLY.
WHO — WHO ARE YOU? WHERE HAVE YOU SPRUNG FROM?
PHEW! I THOUGHT I HAD BOUGHT IT. NEVER THOUGHT I'D BE LUCKY ENOUGH TO HAVE YOU FELLOWS COME ACROSS ME LIKE THAT.
LUCKY YOU MOST CERTAINLY WERE. WE ARE FREE FRENCH AND SPEND A VERY HAPPY TIME BASHING JERRY CONVOYS. JUST COMING BACK FROM A JAUNT WHEN YOU WERE SPOTTED.
YOU CAN THANK MUSSEF REALLY. HIS HAWK LIKE OLD OPTICS SAW THE SUN FLASHING ON THIS. BUT FOR THAT, WE WOULD HAVE GONE SAILING PAST YOU.
SO! IT DID BRING ME LUCK, JUST AS DAD SAID IT WOULD.

Soon—
WAIT! THIS WRITING. JUST WHERE DID YOU GET THIS?
QUITE A STORY BEHIND IT. GOING BACK TO THE LAST WAR AND A FRENCH TOWN GETTING BOMBED BY THE HUNS.
BUT THIS IS INCREDIBLE, THAT STORY YOU TOLD ME.
MAYBE. BUT IT IS AS TRUE AS I SIT HERE, I CAN ASSURE YOU.
I AM LT. ANTON LENARE! AND THE MAN WHO INSCRIBED THIS VERY CASE IS MY UNCLE, SILVERSMITH STILL OF MY HOME TOWN OF RENECOURT.
EH? YOUR UNCLE? BUT THIS IS INCREDIBLE. THE MAN WHO SAVED THAT BOY WITH MY FATHER ALL THOSE YEARS AGO!
AND I AM THAT BOY, MY FRIEND, WHO IS MOST GRATEFUL TO MEET THE SON OF THE MAN THAT SAVED MY LIFE.
Later—
WAIT TILL I TELL DAD ABOUT THIS LITTLE TURN UP!
Four months later—
WHAT A STORY! THEY SAY TRUTH IS STRANGER THAN FICTION AND THIS IS CERTAINLY A CASE OF IT.
HARDLY, DAD. I'D BE MORE INCLINED TO CALL IT A CASE OF COINCIDENCE!
The End

FIGARO!
WE EES OFF TO ROB ZE BANK, PANCHO! HAVE OUR TEA READY FOR US!
OKEYDOKEY!
BUT ONE HOUR LATER...
BAH! YOU FAILED TO ROB ZE BANK AGAIN, FIGARO! YOU EES A HOPELESS BANDIT! WHAT EES YOU?
I EES A HOPELESS BANDIT!
TO TOWN
AH, WELL, AT LEAST ZE RIDE HAVE GIVEN US AN APPETITE! AN' LOOK... GOOD OLD FRYIN' PANCHO EES MAKIN' PANCAKES FOR TEA!
GRUB EES READY.
OH...NO! EET EES ZAT AWFUL FRIED CACTUS!
AGAIN!
FRIED CACTUS, FRIED CACTUS! ALL ZE TIMES EET'S FRIED CACTUS! WE EES OFF TO SURRENDER TO ZE SHERIFF...ZE FOOD EEN JAIL WEEL BE MUCH BETTER!
WAIT! COME BACKS! YOU CANNOT DO ZIS TO ME! YOU NEEDS ME!
HUH! LEAVIN' ME...LIKE RATS FROM A SINKIN' SHEEP-ER-SHIP! BUT I WEEL SHOW ZEM WHO'S BOSS!
I WEEL HEAD ZEM OFF BEFORE ZEY REACH TOWN.
LONG CUT
SHORT CUT
STOPS! I HAS COME TO SHOW YOU WHO EES ZE BOSS!
FIGARO!
TO TOWN
TURN AROUND! YOU EES GOIN' BACK TO ZE CAMP WEETH ME!
TAN ME HIDE! A HOLD-UP!
BETTER GET THE SHERIFF!
AND SO...
THERE HE IS, SHERIFF!
GOT HIM!
COME ON, FELLAH! I'M TAKIN' YOU TO JAIL!
BUT-BUT-SHERIFF, WE WANT TO GO TO JAIL TOO!
PLEASE! PLEASE! TAKE US TO JAIL! PLEASE!
THESE POOR GUYS ARE RAVING! MUST BE DUE TO THE SHOCK OF THE HOLD-UP! I'LL JUST IGNORE THEM!
JAIL
HUH! YOU WAS WRONG ABOUT ZE FOOD BEING BETTER EEN JAIL! EET'S WORSE... BOILED CACTUS!

Two of a Kind!

By 1895, the American Wild West had largely settled down and most of the infamous bands of outlaws had been brought to justice. But one band still remained — that led by Sam "Snake-Eyes" Sawyer and his partner, Seth "Commanche" Kelly . . .
WAITING FOR NED TO COME BACK AND LET US KNOW ABOUT THE RAID ON THAT BANK IS GETTING ME DOWN. I WANT SOME ACTION!
I CAN BELIEVE KELLY WAS BROUGHT UP BY COMMANCHES. HE'S AS MEAN AS ANY BUCK AND NOT THE SORT TO TURN YOUR BACK ON.
Then . . .
YOU SAY HOOTING OWL CREEK'S MINING PAYROLL IS DUE AT NOON. THEN I SAY WE RIDE OVER THERE PRONTO AND CLEAN UP.
WHAT I SAY GOES AROUND HERE, KELLY — NOT YOU!
SEEMS YOU FORGET WHO RUNS THIS BAND. AND ONE DAY I MIGHT JUST GET A BIT TIRED OF HAVING TO REMIND YOU.
HE'S SNAKE FAST WITH THAT GUN. BETTER HUMOUR THE SKUNK. BUT ONE DAY ME AND HIM ARE GOING TO COME TO A SHOWDOWN!
Soon . . .
THIS SHOULD BE ONE OF THE EASIEST JOBS WE'VE HAD FOR SOME TIME. WE CAN HIT THAT BANK FAST AND GET OUT BEFORE THEY KNOW WHAT HIT 'EM.
HOTEL

But suddenly . . .
STOCKMEN'S BANK
DON'T LET THEM GET AWAY!
A TRAP! THAT SKUNK NED MUST HAVE TIPPED THEM OFF. AND WE RODE RIGHT INTO IT!
THEY AINT GOT US YET, KELLY.
AND THIS TINHORN TOWN WON'T, BY THUNDER. EAT LEAD, HOMBRE.
AARGH!
Two weeks later . . .
WE HAVE TO HAVE GRUB AND MONEY, SAWYER. THAT POSSE'S BEEN HUNTING US LIKE WE WERE COYOTES.
WHAT DO YOU THINK I CAN DO? WORK A MIRACLE?
Shortly . . .
SAY! THAT'S SOME PLACE. RECKON THERE COULD WELL BE SOMETHING TO SET A COUPLE OF FELLAHS UP DOWN THERE.
WE'LL WAIT TILL NIGHTFALL, THEN MOSEY ON DOWN. BOUND TO BE PLENTY OF GRUB AND CASH IN A JOINT LIKE THAT.
And so . . .
IT WAS EASY GETTING IN. NOW LET'S JUST SEE IF WE CAN GET THIS SAFE OPEN. SHOULDN'T BE TOO HARD FOR A FELLAH LIKE ME!
JUST GET ON WITH IT AND STOP JAWIN'. THIS PLACE GIVES ME THE CREEPS!
Suddenly . . .
JEST HOLD IT THAR, HOMBRES. ONE WRONG MOVE AND YOU GET IT!
GUARDS. AND THEY'VE GOT US COLD!

WELCOME TO MY HUMBLE ABODE, GENTLEMEN. AND IF I'M NOT MISTAKEN IT HAS BEEN HONOURED BY THE OUTLAWS KELLY AND SAWYER. THE REWARD POSTERS FLATTER YOU.
WHAT KIND OF CREEP IS THIS? HE DON'T LOOK LIKE NO RANCHER I'VE EVER SEEN.
I COULD OF COURSE DO THE RIGHT THING AND HAND YOU OVER TO THE LAW. BUT CYRUS E. TUCKER HAS NEVER BEEN KNOWN FOR DOING THE RIGHT THING.
DARNED IF I CAN FIGURE THIS ALL OUT. BUT WHILE HE'S JAWIN' HE AINT BRINGING IN THE SHERIFF!
I STRUCK IT RICH A COUPLE OF YEARS AGO WITH MY MINE. VERY RICH. RICH ENOUGH TO PURSUE MY PASSION FOR ART WORKS.
YUH MEAN PICTURES AND THAT SORT OF JUNK?
HE'S AS CRAZY AS A BEDBUG!
YOU CAN EACH EARN A COOL 10,000 DOLLARS FOR DOING A LITTLE JOB FOR ME. WHAT DO YOU SAY?
HECK! ENOUGH DOUGH TO GET ACROSS THE BORDER INTO MEXICO — AND GET UP ANOTHER GANG!
Tucker explained . . .
THE NOON STAGE FROM RED BLUFF, REMEMBER. AND YOU KNOW WHAT YOU HAVE TO TAKE FROM IT?
TWO STATUETTES FROM A LITTLE GUY. THEN YOU WANT US TO BRING THEM TO YOU.
REMEMBER. IT MUST BE THE PAIR OR THERE IS NO DEAL. SEPARATE THEY ARE OF NO VALUE TO ME.
DON'T WORRY, HOMBRE. WE WILL GET BOTH OF THEM FOR SURE.

So . . .
RIGHT ON TIME. AND REMEMBER TO MAKE THIS LOOK LIKE SOME ORDINARY HOLD-UP LIKE TUCKER SAID!
IT'S SAWYER AND KELLY. I'M NOT TRYING TO OUTRUN THAT PAIR. THEY CAN HAVE EVERYTHING.
TAKE THEM. TAKE ANYTHING BUT DON'T KILL ME.
LOT OF FUSS OVER THESE THINGS. BUT WITH THE DOUGH WE ARE BEING PAID, WHO CARES?
LET'S SEE ONE OF THOSE THINGS. UGLY LITTLE CRITTURS IF YOU ASK ME.
I DIDN'T. NOW GET THAT STRONG BOX DOWN OFF THE STAGE!
Meanwhile . . .
SOON THE DIACHANG TWINS SHALL BE MINE. THAT FOOL SMITHERS SHOULD NOT HAVE VISITED ME AND BOASTED HE HAD THEM, FOR BY NOW HE WILL NOT HAVE THEM! HAW! HAW! HAW!
But . . .
LOOK! OUTLAWS! IF JASPER'S MOUNT HADN'T THROWN HIM WE WOULD HAVE GOT 'EM COLD.
HECK! LOOKS LIKE THIS STAGE HAD AN ESCORT. LET'S GET OUT OF HERE!

HEAD FOR RED ROCK IF WE GET SEPARATED, SAWYER.
CURSE IT! HE HAS ONE OF THOSE THINGS. AND UNLESS THEY ARE A PAIR THEY ARE WORTH NOTHING TO US.
GET THEM. THEY MUST NOT ESCAPE WITH THE DIACHANG TWINS!
ARGHHHH! MY HORSE IS DOWN!
I'M NOT STOPPING WITH THAT ESCORT RIGHT BEHIND — AS MUCH AS I WANT THAT STATUE.
THEY SPLIT UP! I'LL FOLLOW THE LEFT SET OF TRACKS WITH JASPER'S BUNCH TAKING THE RIGHT!
I JEST HOPE THEY DON'T GET SAWYER. IT'LL KIND OF RUIN EVERYTHING IF THEY SPLIT THE STATUES.
A week later in Red Rock . . .
SO, KELLY GAVE THEM THE SLIP. I JEST HOPE HE STILL HAS THAT STATUE.
SAWYER! I MIGHT HAVE KNOWN THAT WILY RANGE RAT WOULD DODGE ANY POSSE. I JEST HOPE HE STILL HAS THAT STATUE.
SO, YOU HAVE THE THING STASHED. WHATSAY YOU COME UP TO MY CABIN WITH IT THIS AFTERNOON? AND AFTER A BITE TO EAT WE GO AND SEE TUCKER.
SOUNDS OKAY BY ME. YOU STILL HAVE THAT CABIN UP IN THE REDPINE ROCKS THEN?
Shortly . . .
COME ON, YOU LITTLE MONSTER. YOU AND YOUR CHUM ARE GOING TO MAKE ME A RICH MAN.
REAL STROKE OF LUCK US GOING TO ROB THAT PLACE, KELLY. WHAT THAT FELLAH WILL PAY US FOR THESE TWO WILL SET US UP REAL GOOD.
TOO TRUE. LET'S HAVE A DRINK TO CELEBRATE. HELP YOURSELF WHILE I GET ANOTHER GLASS!

JUST THINK. 10,000 DOLLARS EACH.
BUT JUST THINK. IF ANYTHING HAPPENED TO YOU, PARDNER, MY SHARE WOULD BE 20,000 DOLLARS — WHICH IS EVEN BETTER.
ARGHHHH!
PITY ABOUT THAT. WE WERE TWO OF A KIND YOU AND ME, KELLY. BUT WE JUST RODE THE LAST TRAIL TOGETHER.
HERE'S TO MEXICO. AND A NEW SAWYER GANG. ADIOS, AMIGO.
ARGHHHH! THE WHISKEY. THAT SKUNK POISONED IT! HE DOUBLE-CROSSED ME!
Like the Diachang Twins, Kelly and Sawyer were two of a kind!
The End

WINGS OF WAR
Carrier pigeons were used by both sides in the First World War, before wireless was reliable for sending messages, especially in the field of espionage. One of the few German spies who worked in England for a time was Albert Schwartz, better known as Alf Black, who lived near a big naval port on the East Coast.
MORNING, MAJOR, SIR. I GOT A NICE SELECTION OF HOMERS FOR YOU TODAY. ALL FRESH AND TRAINED, ME OWN HOME BREEDING, OF COURSE. NOTHING BUT THE BEST FOR THE CARRIER PIGEON SERVICE!
GOOD SHOW, BLACK! WE RELY ON YOU CHAPS TO SUPPLY US WITH FIRST RATE STOCK. I'LL HAVE MY MAN FETCH THE BASKETS TO THE CAR.
HURRY UP, DUNTHORP!
THE QUICKER THEY GO THE BETTER! I MUST HURRY OR I SHALL BE LATE FOR THE RENDEZVOUS! OFFICIAL PIGEON BREEDER TO H. M. GOVERNMENT! ACH, LITTLE DO THE POMPOUS FOOLS KNOW!
That night, somewhere on the coast —
GOOD, THEY ARE COMING!
HIMMEL, I WILL BE GLAD TO BE GONE FROM HERE!
WE MEET AGAIN, SCHWARTZ. GOOD LUCK! THE FATHERLAND NEEDS EVERY SCRAP OF INFORMATION YOU CAN SEND!
DANKE, HERR LEUTNANT! I WILL DO MY BEST, BE SURE!

Back at the yard —
SAFELY BACK WITH FRESH HOMING BIRDS TO CARRY MESSAGES TO GERMANY! I MUST SETTLE THEM INTO THE LOFT BEFORE ANYTHING ELSE.
HELLO, MISTER. YOU BEEN FLYIN' 'EM?
YOU STARTLED ME, JOHNNY! FLYING? OH, ER, NO, NO! JUST A BIT OF A CHANGE ROUND.
I AIN'T NEVER SEEN THAT ONE BEFORE, MISTER. WHERE DID YOU GET IT?
ER — NOWHERE, BOY. I'VE HAD IT FOR AGES. A YEAR AT LEAST. NOW BUZZ OFF, I'M BUSY!
DUMKOPF BOY! I HATE IT WHEN THEY GET INQUISITIVE! I WONDER HOW MUCH HE TOOK IN? I'VE BEEN HERE TOO LONG TO GIVE MYSELF AWAY! BETTER GET OUT AND SEE WHAT I CAN OBSERVE NOW.
Shortly —
YES, PLENTY OF MOVEMENT. I RECOGNISE MOST OF THE SHIPS. A BIT MORE DETAIL FROM CARELESS TALK AND I SHALL KNOW WHEN SHIPS ARE LEAVING ON PATROL.
Suddenly —
HIMMEL! A POLICEMAN!

GOOD DAY. A HANDSOME VIEW, EH?
INDEED IT IS, OFFICER. AND A SPLENDID PLACE AT WHICH TO GIVE THE OLD HORSE A BREATHER.
OH, NO! IT'S TOSSED OUT THE BINOCULARS!
PHEW! THAT WAS CLOSE!
Alf Black turned for home, and presently . . .
WHAT ARE YOU DOING, BOY? YOU HAD NO RIGHT TO COME IN! I DO NOT PERMIT ANYONE ELSE NEAR MY BIRDS! CLEAR OFF! GO!
I-I'M SORRY, MISTER. I WAS ONLY TRYIN' TO HELP LIKE!
HE'S A RIGHT PAIN! I WASN'T DOIN' NO HARM. I'LL SHOW HIM!
Later —
. . . ABOVE SHIPS IN HARBOUR, DUE TO SAIL WITHIN 48 HOURS FROM TIME OF DISPATCH. SUGGEST URGENT STEPS BE TAKEN TO STOP THIS TASK FORCE WHICH IS RUMOURED TO THREATEN PORTS ON THE NORTH GERMAN COAST. MESSAGE ENDS.

I'VE PICKED THE STRONGEST-LOOKING BIRD FOR THE JOB. IT IS TOO IMPORTANT TO TAKE CHANCES. I MUST GET WORD OFF AS SOON AS POSSIBLE.
HE'S OFF AGAIN. I MUST HAVE ANOTHER LOOK AT THOSE PIGEONS, THEY'RE GREAT. HE WON'T KNOW I'VE BEEN IN.
Later —
NO ONE ABOUT! FLY TRUE, FRAULEIN!
Meanwhile —
THE PIEBALD BIRD HAS GONE! HE MUST HAVE TAKEN IT WITH HIM IN HIS KNAPSACK! WONDER WHAT FOR? NOT RACING, THAT'S FOR SURE. IT AIN'T ALLOWED.
Next day —
HE'S OFF! I'M GOIN' IN TO SEE TO THEM BIRDS WHETHER HE LIKES IT OR NOT! I'LL CLEAN 'EM OUT. HE'LL NEVER KNOW!
POOR THINGS HAVE RUN OUT OF GRIT. I'LL SEE IF THERE'S SOME IN THE SHED.

LOCKED! THE WINDOW'S NOT FASTENED THOUGH. I'LL NIP IN THAT WAY. THE PIGEONS HAVE GOT TO HAVE GRIT FOR THEIR CROPS.
THERE'S THE GRIT! I CAN REACH IT FROM HERE.
CRIKEY, THAT'S TORN IT! I'LL HAVE TO CLEAR THE MESS UP NOW!
HE'D GO MAD IF HE FOUND ME HERE MAKING A MESS LIKE THIS! FUNNY, HE DIDN'T SEEM TO MIND MUCH WHEN I FIRST STARTED COMING TO SEE THE PIGEONS. THEN HE DIDN'T SEEM TO WANT TO ANSWER ME QUESTIONS. I'M GOING TO KEEP PIGEONS OF ME OWN ONE DAY!
GRIT
THAT'S DONE. NOW I'D BETTER — HEY, WHAT'S THAT?
HOLY SMOKE! EVEN I KNOW THAT'S GERMAN! WHAT'S HE UP TO?

I CAN HARDLY BELIEVE IT! IF THAT'S GERMAN IT MEANS THE BLOKE WHO KEEPS THE PIGEONS IS WRITING MESSAGES FOR 'EM TO CARY! THAT'S WHY HE WENT OFF WITH A KNAPSACK AND THE PIEBALD BIRD IS MISSING! I'M GETTING OUT OF HERE BEFORE HE COMES BACK!
Johnny took his fears to the police —
IT MAY BE NOTHING, YOU SEE, BUT — WELL, I THINK MISTER BLACK GOT A NEW PIGEON THE OTHER DAY, AND NOW IT'S GONE, AND I FOUND THE WRITING, AND —
OH AR, HIM, EH? YOU THINK HE'S A SPY, HUH? WELL NOW, WAIT 'ERE, LAD. I'LL HAVE A WORD.
Johnny was taken to meet an army captain —
— AND THAT'S ALL I KNOW, SIR. BUT I THOUGHT THERE'S SOMETHING FISHY ABOUT IT, AND HE WAS NASTY WHEN I LOOKED AT HIS BIRDS, SENT ME PACKIN'. I ONLY WANTED TO HELP. I LOVE PIGEONS, HONEST.
QUITE SO. HRRRMPH! YES, YES, YOUNG MAN. WORTH LOOKIN' INTO! WE'LL KEEP YOU POSTED. MANY THANKS! OFF YOU GO NOW, AND MUM'S THE WORD, MIND!
Shortly —
ALFRED BLACK, YOU ARE WANTED FOR QUESTIONING IN CONNECTION WITH ESPIONAGE CHARGES, UNDER THE DEFENCE OF THE REALM ACT.
IT IS AN OUTRAGE! I AM INNOCENT!
Later that day —
ACTION STATIONS!
It was 48 hours after Albert Schwartz's message —
THEY ARE LEAVING HARBOUR NOW! THESE MUST BE THE SHIPS WE ARE TO ATTACK. THE BRITISH TASK FORCE! PREPARE TORPEDOES!
JAWOHL, HERR KAPITAN!

But suddenly —
HIMMEL! DIVE, DIVE!
TOO LATE! THEY'VE HOLED THE PRESSURE HULL! WE'RE SINKING!
COME ON, FRITZ, UPS-A-DAISY. WAR'S OVER FOR YOU.
Sometime later —
AIM! FIRE!
Meanwhile —
I'M SURE THAT'S ONE OF THE NEW ONES. LOOK, IT'S GOT A SEVEN WITH A LINE THROUGH IT AMONG THE NUMBERS TATTOOED ON ITS WING.
HE'S RIGHT, SIR. CONTINENTAL SEVEN.
JOVE YES! WELL, THAT GIVES US FIVE BIRDS THAT WILL HOME TO THE HUNS. WE CAN SEND FALSE INFORMATION THAT COULD LURE U-BOATS OR ZEPPELINS TO WHERE OUR CHAPS CAN DESTROY THEM! THANKS TO YOU, YOUNG MAN. AND AFTER THAT YOU CAN CARRY ON LOOKING AFTER THE REST OF THE PIGEONS, IF YOU LIKE. HOW ABOUT IT, EH?
There was not much doubt about Johnny's whoop of delight. It was all the answer the Major needed!